PORTRAIT OF A SMALL TOWN

PORTRAIT OF A SMALL TOWN

A PICTORIAL AND PERSONAL HISTORY OF HUNTINGTON STATION

ALFRED V. SFORZA

Printed in the United States of America
First Edition

ISBN 0-930545-16-8

CONTENTS

DEDICATION

This book is dedicated to my parents, Lena and Fred Sforza. They gave me my past; they made my present possible; and they said that the future is my responsibility.

ACKNOWLEDGEMENTS

Many thanks to all those who helped me, and those who inspired or provided their memories for this book:

My parents, who gave me life and the courage and determination to pursue my goals; Mitzi Caputo, for always being cheerfully available to climb two flights of stairs to find me "just one more photograph;" Florence Bowes, for just being herself, and for constantly pursuing the search for someone else to interview; Leon Gimpel; Eugene Ligotti; Robert Gottlieb; Herbert Haas; Sam Lewis; Harold Jacobson, Christian Jacobsen and Karen Jacobsen Bosak; Andy Coscia; John LoScalzo; Laurette Lamberta Prisco; Marge Van Velsor Osburn and Joe Osburn; Margaret & Stan Van Velsor; Edward Hoag; Ray DeVine; Frank Roselle; Vincent and Phyllis Gigante; Bill Amadio; Edward Johntry; Beatrice Teich; June Hess Kelly; Jack Abrams, curator of the Huntington District Heritage Museum; Francis "Tim" McElwein, my high school history teacher; John Hulsen (1898-1988), who started my collection of photographs; and my office staff, who had to listen to these stories over and over again.

Special thanks to my wife, Barbara, for tolerating the hours I spent sitting at the computer.

—AVS

INTRODUCTION

The most frequent question asked me while I was working on this book was, "Why are you writing about Huntington Station?" For a long time now, it has been considered "the other side of the tracks." I thought it was time someone told our story.

One day, while walking through what used to be our bustling community near the railroad station, I watched the wind blow over a dusty parking lot. Leaves, jumping in swirling circles above the pavement, reminded me of the happy children who used to skip along the sidewalks there. Now commuters, known as "Dashing Dans," were running to catch their trains. Preoccupied with their new business day in New York City, they probably gave little thought to the history of the ground they were running over. Many were totally unaware that a small town had once existed on this spot. How could they know? When one visualizes New York City, there are familiar landmarks associated with it — the Empire State Building, the Twin Towers — but few buildings remain to testify that this part of Huntington Station was once a thriving community.

Old houses and buildings have an unfortunate way of disappearing, sometimes by wear and tear, sometimes through neglect. In this case, the death of the community was precipitated by a project called "urban renewal." The goal of urban renewal was to revitalize the Huntington Station area. The plan was to tear down and rebuild, and to give the existing businesses first preference to the new stores. (I don't know where those businesses were expected to go during the destruction-construction phase.) During the mid-1960's, urban renewal started systematically destroying the buildings and displacing the businesses. They soon realized that there was no money left to rebuild. A $29-million-dollar project, and no money to continue. Not even a "sorry" to all the shopkeepers displaced. No apology to the residents. Not even a plaque to show that this was the former site of our community.

I stared at the sad, empty spaces, shaking my head in disbelief, and thought of all the people and stores that used to line New York Avenue. I wanted to go home again. The thought came to me that it would be nice to walk through the old town and see all the people again—a kind of "Back to the Future" for Huntington Station.

My desire to write this book was many-fold. By assembling photographs and personal reminiscences, I hoped that the image of what Huntington Station had been would emerge. Ours was a wonderful town, and we will never forget what it meant to us. By knowing and remembering what used to be, one gains a better understanding of what *can* be. Hopefully, the errors of the past will not be repeated. If history is any guide, what happened in Huntington Station could happen to other small communities. We should take the initiative and prevent them from crumbling due to lack of interest, or worse yet, from the feeling that it could not happen elsewhere.

While I first began to collect photographs of Huntington Station, I discovered that many of them were taken after urban renewal had started to tear the community apart and it had begun to look like a skeleton of its former self. I realized that the photographs were not going to tell the whole story of the town. I had to find another approach. Something was missing. People!

The history of communities is about ordinary people at work and play. The events in the lives of the people who lived in the town would give life and meaning to my collection of inanimate photographs. Although not many people remain who remember the community at its best, these few were my only way to recapture the true meaning of Huntington Station.

I was not prepared for their enthusiasm and their willingness to share their experiences. Through my interviews I exchanged ideas and memories with many people of different backgrounds and generations, and they all had the same pride in being part of the history of our small town.

Some of the old photographs I collected helped me to get each person's memory working. Gradually, the image of our community started to emerge. Many stories told to me were the kind that parents and grandparents tell children while sitting around a campfire or the kitchen table—the stories we hear time and again until we're bored or embarrassed. But throughout all my interviews, I never felt that way. Each story was important because it was a first-hand report of what had happened yesterday. They are valuable links to our past. The more stories we can record, the easier it will be for the younger generation to share in the memories of those who have lived in our town. My only regret is that I didn't start soon enough. I never questioned my grandparents about their coming to America; all their memories are lost forever. My advice to the younger generation is to ask questions, listen, and record your family history.

In writing this book, I had the unique experience of reliving part of my life and the lives of others. Even if only on paper, I could once again walk down the streets of our community, see the buildings and talk with the people who used to be there. Come with me and visit old Huntington Station, my kind of town.

THE HUNTINGTON HISTORICAL SOCIETY

The Huntington Historical Society was organized in 1903 as a part of the Town of Huntington's celebration of its 250th anniversary (1653-1903). Through the years, the Society has been the leader in collecting and preserving the history of our town. Membership in this nonprofit educational organization is open to the public.

According to the bylaws, the object of the organization "shall be to *preserve the heritage* of the Town of Huntington by *maintaining a museum* where objects about Huntington history and life may be preserved and displayed; by *maintaining a research library* relevant to Huntington history; by stimulating interest in the *preservation of buildings or sites that are of historic value*; and by interesting the residents of the Town in the history of Huntington."

Raising sufficient operating funds has always been difficult for the Huntington Historical Society. To stay in existence, the Society depends on extremely dedicated volunteers, too many to mention by name, who help a small professional staff. Recently, due to a financial crisis, most of the paid staff was furloughed, some after many years of service. The dedication of these workers is such that some of them have returned, now *volunteering* their much-needed services. These are the kind of people whom you will meet when you visit the Museums, Museum Shop, and Library.

209 Main Street, Huntington

Files of material covering many subjects concerning local history, social life and customs have expanded over the years through the generosity of donors. Available in the collection on microfilm is *The Long Islander,* a local newspaper founded by Walt Whitman, with issues from 1839 to the present. In addition, there are wills, the Federal Census of Suffolk County 1790-1880, deeds, maps, atlases, gazetteers, business records, and over 30,000 photographs.

The Huntington Historical Society has the important responsibility of preserving our Town's history, and has a collection of irreplaceable items. Even the basement, stacked almost to the ceiling with documents and photographs, has the musty scent of generations gone by. Preserving our history is significant in giving life-long residents a sense of belonging and newer residents a sense of *wanting* to belong.

Photographs and illustrations used in this book, and not identified as being from other collections, are courtesy of the Huntington Historical Society. A special thank you for the helpful assistance, constant encouragement, and invaluable knowledge of Mitzi Caputo.

PART I

HISTORY

THE SETTLEMENT OF THE HUNTINGTON AREA

It would be impossible to rebuild an image of Huntington Station without first discussing the origin of Huntington itself. There were probably several thousand Native Americans living on Long Island when the first Dutch and English settlers arrived. The first explorers to the "New World," thinking they had arrived in India, called these Native Americans *Indians.* The Indians were divided into groups headed by a chief, and occupied defined territories. Stones, streams and trails marked the boundary of a territory. Neighboring tribes respected these boundaries, and did not violate them to hunt or fish. Trouble with the settlers might have been avoided had the new settlers respected the boundary laws.

Wall painting at Chase Bank in Huntington

The Matinecocks were the tribe that inhabited the Huntington region. Their territory extended from Flushing Bay to the Nissequogue River at Smithtown. The Indian name for the area we know as Huntington Village was *Ketewomoke,* meaning "where the sea flows." It is difficult to locate the exact spot where the name originally applied, due to the fact that the Matinecock tribe roamed about and gave the name to many places, perhaps far from where they originated. The tribe consisted of about 30 families. In general, they were peaceful with neighboring tribes and the new settlers.

A painting on the wall of the Chase (Chemical) Bank—now at the corner of Woodbury Road and Main Street, and formerly Security National Bank—is H. Willard Ortlip's conception of the Matinecocks witnessing the arrival of the first European settlers. Neither the Indians nor the newcomers could foresee the changes that would transform their territory into the busy suburb we know today.

What a struggle for existence it was for the settlers! They must have dreaded the approach of the long cold winters. Heating their homes and getting and storing food were ongoing concerns. They would certainly not have survived without the friendly assistance of the Indians. They introduced the settlers to new foods—the most important was corn—and showed them Indian methods of planting, including using dead fish as fertilizer for crops. Indians also taught the settlers how to hunt, trap, snare rabbits, fish, and even shared their food with them. In the woods and fields was an abundance of fruits and berries. With this new-found knowledge, the settlers survived the long winters.

Indian words still echo throughout Long Island today, in the names of towns and places. Here are some examples of Indian words and their meanings:

1. Asharokan —the name of the chief of the Matinecocks
2. Montauk — "a place for seeing far off"
3. Massapequa — "land on the great cove"
4. Shinnecock (Bay) — "a level country"
5. Peconic (Bay) — "a small plantation"
6. Ketewomoke (Yacht Club) — "where the sea flows," "the shore" or "beach"
7. Comac (Commack) — from the word "winnecomac," meaning "pleasant land" or "good land"

The identity of Huntington as a town began on April 2, 1653. Three men from Oyster Bay came down Cold Spring Hill along the trail known as Oyster Bay Path (which is Main Street today), looking to buy some land from the Indians. These three — Richard Houlbrook, Robert Williams and Daniel Whitehead — bargained with the chief of the Matinecocks. Having been at many real estate closings, I wish I could have been present at *this* discussion with the Indians — not only for the historic event, but also to see how they bargained with a few coats and shirts, a few implements, and "six fathoms of wampum" for this land. In reading over the 1887 translation of the agreement, I wonder what would have happened if the Chief had had his own lawyer.

This agreement is known as "The Old First Purchase." The area was bounded on the west by Cold Spring Harbor, on the north by Long Island Sound, on the east by Northport Harbor, and extended south approximately to Old Country Road. A plaque was erected honoring the first purchase and can be seen on the corner of Old Country Road and Route 110.

The following is an 1887 translation of the deed of 1653, by Charles R. Street. It appeared in *Our Town, Huntington 1653-1953 A Tercentenary Commemoration.*

Articles of Agreement betwixt Raseokan sagamore of Matinecock of the one part, and Richard Houldbrock, Robert Williams, Danial Whitehead, of the other party, witnesseth as followeth:

Know all men whome these present writing(s) may any where concerne that I Raseokan do sell & make over unto the aforesaid parties Richard Houldbrock, Robart Williams & Daniel Whitehead, their heirs, executors or assigns, a certain quantitie of land, lying and being on Long Island, Bounded upon the West side with a river commonly called by the Indians Nachaquetack, on the North side with the sea and going eastward to a river called Opcatkontycke, on the south to the utmost of my bounds; promising, and by virtue herof I do promise to free the above lands from all title off and claim that shall be made unto it by reason of any former act: in consideration of which land the aforesaid Richard Houldbrock, Robart Williams and Danial Whitehead doth promise unto the said Raseokan as followeth: 6 coats, 6 kettles, 6 hatchets, 6 howes, 6 shirts, 10 knives, 6 fathom of wampum, 30 muxes, 30 needles, further the said sachem doth promise to go or send someone in twenty days to show & mark out the bounds & in case it prove not acording to expectation then this writing to be voyde & of none efectt, but in case it be, then this writing to stand in full force, power and virtue. Witness our hands the 2th of April 1653.

The mark of
Richard X. Houlbrock,
Robard Williams,
Daniell Whitehead

the X mark of the sagamore
the mark X of Heworkes
the mark X of Muhama
the mark X of Syhar
20 other marks by Raseokan tribesmen

This is the true coppe of the
origenall deed
witnes our hands

Thomas Richards
Moses Iohnson
Recorded in the office at New Yorke 11th
day of November 1667
Matthias Nicholls, sec'r.

The difficulty in reviewing historical documents is trying to understand what is meant by the many misspelled words. Often, different recorders have various spellings of the same names and places. Correct spelling in our early records of Huntington was also difficult because the Indians had no written language and the early settlers wrote the names phonetically. Therefore no two recorders were likely to spell the names exactly the same. As a result, the name of the chief of the Matinecocks as written on the first deed was *Chief Raseokan;* he was later referred to as *Chief Asharokan.* Also, the name Houlbrook changes to Houldbrock, Houldbrook, Houldbroke and Holbrook, depending on which source is used.

While we are on the subject of old records, it is important to note that in addition to the Huntington Historical Society, our present town clerk, JoAnn Raia, had the official opening of "The Town Clerk's Archives" on May 12, 1995. Through her efforts, grants were obtained, and many of the early official records of the Town of Huntington have been collected and preserved. Except for some records that are too fragile, they are accessible for examination by researchers, providing they receive permission from the Town Clerk and Records Management Officer.

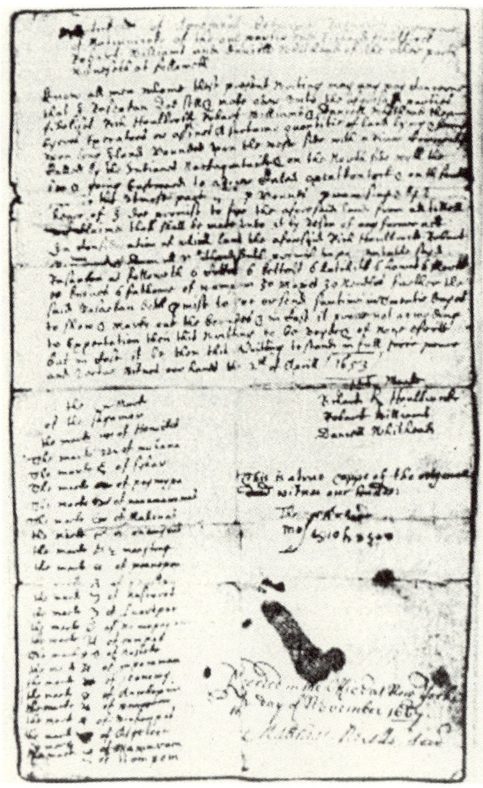

First Purchase Deed, 1653

The Indians did not put great importance on the accumulation of material possessions and had very different ideas concerning the ownership of property than did the settlers. Unfortunately, this led to misunderstandings when the first settlers purchased their lands. The Indians did not realize that such purchases were binding for all time, but considered them as we do a lease. Occasionally, to keep peace, the settlers found it wise to make a second payment.

Three years later, on July 30, 1656, a second or "Eastern Purchase" was made from the same tribe and extended the town's boundary eastward to Smithtown. These deeds also caused Lloyd Neck to be part of Oyster Bay until June 15, 1866. At that time, by petition of the residents, it was annexed to Huntington. In 1872, the Town of Huntington was divided, and the southern portion became the Town of Babylon.

There are many theories as to why the first European settlers renamed the territory from Ketewomoke to Huntington, but it is generally agreed that they named it in honor of Oliver Cromwell, who was born in Huntingdon, Huntingdonshire, England. Our old Town records show that they did originally spell the name with a "d" and later substituted the "t."

Today, the 94 square miles of the Town of Huntington, on Long Island Sound in northwestern Suffolk County, has a population of over 200,000. The villages include Asharoken, Centerport, Cold Spring Harbor, Commack (part in Smithtown), Dix Hills, East Northport, Eaton's Neck, Elwood, Fort Salonga (part in Smithtown), Greenlawn, Halesite, Huntington, Huntington Bay, Huntington Station, Lloyd Harbor, Melville, Northport, South Huntington, USCG Station at Eaton's Neck, and West Hills.

Many old roads used by the settlers followed the trails the Indians used to go into the hills where hunting provided them with food and clothing. The road leading south from the village was called South Road and was eventually called New York Avenue. Approximately two miles south of Huntington Village is where Huntington Station eventually flourished.

OLD TOWN SEAL
authorized by the Dongan Patent 1688. The "E" indicated the fifth town in the official British records.

Granted in 1688, the Dongan Patent, (named after New York's Lieutenant Governor) confirmed the purchase from the Indians of the lands comprising Huntington.

The Long Island Indians had somewhat darker complexions than did most of the Europeans. They were generally tall and well-built, having firm muscles and broad faces. They are described as often showing rather severe expressions on their faces and being able to exercise great control over their emotions by not showing evidence of pain or fear. Their eyes were dark and their hair, which was often treated with bear grease, grew perfectly straight. The braves removed most of the hair from their heads, except for a strip about two inches in width, that extended from forward on the crown to the back of the neck. Part of this was often allowed to grow longer than the rest and was known as the scalp lock, which the braves wore in defiance of their enemies. They sometimes wore one or two feathers, but never the feathered war bonnet. These Indians were unusually strong and could endure great physical hardship without complaining.

From "**The Long Island Indian**"
by Robert R. Coles

One evening we were having dinner with our friends Eugene and Corbina LoScalzo Ligotti. We started a conversation about what the chief of the Matinecock tribe might have said if he came to the future and saw all the changes that had occurred in the area he called his home. The following narrative is Dr. Ligotti's thought-provoking interpretation of an imaginary conversation with the chief in 1653, *the year they signed the treaty,* 1953, *the year of Huntington's Tercentenary Celebration, and* 1996, *long after urban renewal had changed Huntington Station forever.*

I found him standing alone on a hilltop over looking the bay. He was silent and still. Beams of light from the slowly setting sun set his body ablaze and shimmering in a golden glow. Looking like a bronze god in the dusk of the day, he was dressed only in a loincloth, with feathers and beads in his hair, moccasins on his feet, and a bright necklace of shells upon his chest. He wore little paint except that which symbolized him as the sachem of his tribe. Had I found Raseokan, the chief of the peaceful Matinecock Indians? Once a great warrior chieftain against his Iroquois enemies to the north, he now found that prudence was indeed the better part of valor, as his tribe had been cut down not by his enemies, but by a disease he believed was sent by an evil spirit. Was this the great Algonquin chief who also kept the peace with his friend to the east, Wyandance, leader of the tribe called Montauks? He stood before me as silent as a statue. I knew his instincts were keen and that he was aware of my presence. Gingerly I approached and began to speak.

"Are you Raseokan of the Matinecocks? Are you the one who has been dealing with the white men from Oyster Bay?"

"Yes, I am chief sagamore of the Matinecock tribe of the people of the Algonquin nation. True, I and Heworkes, Muhama, Sylar, and other tribesmen placed our marks upon the paper of the white men, Houlbrock, Williams, and Whitehead," said the impressive Indian. I could see that he was looking at my clothing.

"You appear different from other white men. Your hair is shorter and your clothes different. Are you of a different tribe?"

"Not really. I come from the future — yours and mine. I live on this land, a bit inland from here in a place now named Huntington Station. I have seen a village there. Is that where you live?"

"Yes, I live on the land you call Huntington Station. To me and the members of my tribe this land is simply Ketewomoke."

"The white men say the paper you marked—it is called a deed—gives them Ketewomoke."

"What you say is wrong! The paper is wrong! I cannot give that which I do not own. The white men say that we do not understand the concept of ownership. We do. This is my knife. This is my tomahawk. These are my moccasins. They speak of owning the land. It is they who do not understand the concept of dominion. You cannot own land. It belongs to Manitou, the Great Creator. He alone allows us to use the land, to live upon it, to hunt, fish, and pick berries. The white man gives my people many things: coats, kettles, knives, hatchets, and other items including six fathom of wampum. All this for the use of the land."

"What is a fathom? How big is it? Is it the same as we measure the depth of water?"

"A fathom of wampum measures from the tip of the little finger to the elbow. I find it amusing when dealing with the white man and trading wampum for hatchets and the like, their forearms differ in size depending on whether they are giving or getting. We value these belts of beads because they are so difficult to make from the hard shells of the conch, the quahog clam, and the whelk. We exchanged them as gifts and use wampum in ceremonies between our tribes. The white man has created an acceptance of wampum, by trying to place it as equal value with the land. They call it money. Of this I have no concept. I accept these as gifts from friend to friend. I will allow the white men to live on the land, but it is not his nor mine to give. It belongs to, and comes from, the munificence of the Great Spirit. They may use the land for a period of time we have yet to decide upon. We Matinecocks are a peaceful people and these white men have come in peace. We must teach them how to live on the land, for with their meager knowledge they will surely die. There is enough for all and we will share with them as they, I am sure, will share with us. Paper or no paper, we will always be able to hunt and fish on Manitou's land."

Artist's conception of an Indian village on Long Island.

"Great chief, your demeanor tells me that you are depressed. Do you find this trade you have made with the white man troubling?"

"It is an emotion, a passion that I cannot explain. I believe that I have lost something, but I know not what. Our dealings with the white man have always been peaceful, but yet the Great Spirit speaks to me of sadness for my people. White men and their families have come here to live and with our help they will flourish on this land. What has changed is that they now come with papers to mark; a deed you say they call it? Why do they feel it necessary? You are from the future so you must have the answers. What will become of my people? Surely there is enough for all on this great land. Even tens of thousands of moons from now, the land will be as it is now. It has not changed since the beginning of time. This great island has an abundance of all that we and the white man will ever need. The brooks and streams are filled with clear sweet drinking water. The air is healthy and the soil rich for planting. The forests are filled with deer and other animals for the hunt.

"The seas abound with fish and shellfish of all kinds; all ours for the taking. The soil is fertile for farming the food we need for the long winter. Surely the land will remain the same. People of all nations will live together in harmony in a community; the community you call Huntington Station. Several suns have come and gone since I and others have made our marks on the paper, and still the Great Spirit will not give me peace within my soul. But perhaps that is his sign. Since the marks were made, nothing has changed. My people still hunt and fish. The children play. The paper has changed nothing! This is a time of happiness, for the harsh winter is behind us. It is spring and the weather is warm, but still a cold wind blows within my heart. Assure me, friend, that the paper cannot change the land. I feel that I can trust the white man, although this feeling tells me that I am powerless to stop the changes that will come. How and from where I do not know, but my heart tells me that the land will survive as I know it and as I see it now."

He stood immobile and a contentment came into his heart, softening his features. Raising his arm, he pointed to the sea and swept his hand around the horizon, turning slowly until he was once again where he had begun. The great chieftain knew I had not left him. He spoke without looking at me; seemingly speaking not only to me, but to all who would live on this land.

"Life is a circle and if the land must change, so be it. In time the land will be once again as it is now—for the land, like tomorrow, is forever."

My thoughts turned inward and I wondered. Did we do well? Did we treat the land with as much respect as he did?

Raseokan sensed my uneasiness. "Tell me my feelings are not wrong. Tell me the land will survive as I see it now."

"There will be changes," I said hesitantly. "Man's progress toward an unknown future is determined by his ability to master that unknown. New ways, new methods and new ideas will lead the way to inventions, progress, and a general upward movement for mankind."

"And the land? Do not tell me that this progress you speak of will be at the expense of the land! Must I remind you that we are like the animals. Without our natural environment, the land, the water, the air, all as you see it now, mankind will wither and die. How can the land change? You come from the future. Take me there and show me these changes you speak of."

"Yes, I can take you there now, but first I will show you how the white man developed the land and grew. How he made it a flourishing community."

We stood on the railroad crossing over New York Avenue just as a train roared into the station. I saw Raseokan set his jaw as his hand moved to the knife at his belt. He had not flinched or moved away from the sight, which to him was a frightening apparition from some forgotten childhood dream.

"Have no fear, my friend. Nothing can harm you. We cannot be seen. There are many strange sights that I have to show you. This is the year 1953—three hundred years after you made your mark on the white man's paper. We are looking toward the veritable heart of Huntington Station, its shopping district. The white man did flourish as you predicted and they have a fine community. As you can see, the Indian trails have become roads. Horses are now used only for sport. Men travel in cars and trains like the one you saw, and there—look in the sky. We call that a plane. It would take too long to explain how this all came about, but we are here to see the people and how they live. This is the very place were your village once stood. Let me take you to a typical street here in Huntington Station. You will see, and I am sure that you will be pleased that the people still live in harmony on this great land."

I took him to one of the many streets where the people lived in unity, friendship, and kindliness. He saw healthy children playing, much the same as the Indian children played here three hundred years ago. We walked together down an old Indian trail now widened and called New York Avenue. He was gladdened as he saw store after store of merchants selling their wares and services. All harmoniously working together. He was pleased.

"The people still use the land wisely as a community of good will. Friendly, happy children are at play. Their parents appear content. But where are my people? Where are the Indians?"

"There are still many Indians. This country is vast and the Indians, now numbering many more than when you walked this land, live in different parts of the country. I am sorry to say that some tribes no longer exist, but others flourish in this great nation."

"I am pleased. Is there more of this future that you can show me?"

"Yes, we now go to the present year, 1996."

We stood at the same spot over looking New York Avenue. Raseokan glanced around him. All he could see was parking lots and roadways. He turned to me and his pleasant demeanor had changed to one of shock.

"Only 43 years since last I looked, and now there is massive change. The land is covered with what you have called asphalt and concrete. You force an ever-dwindling number of trees to grow through holes in the stone. Where is the village and the community? Where are the shops and stores, the area you called the veritable heart of Huntington Station? Where do the people live? I sense that all the deer and other wildlife have gone from this place. The beautiful streams and brooks are dried and gone. Your air and water are fouled. What destruction will come in the next 43 years? When will the circle of life return the land to the people? Please take me farther into the future. Let me see the full circle."

I attempted to divert him. "I can show you other areas, some far north and west of here and in other states, where the air is still clear and the water pure. The land is relatively untouched and..."

"No! This was my home. I lived here!"

A tear coursed its way down his cheek and he was silent. I reached for his shoulder and he moved away, almost fearful of my touch. I could feel and sympathize with his sadness.

"I understand..."

"You do not understand. I have seen enough. Take me back. Leave me with my fears, but without memory of this abomination of what your future has done to the land!"

I took him back and, as promised, left him without memory of our trip into the future which I then knew was caused by each and every one of us, by our complacency, insufficient insight or lack of action. I left him content with the land he knew and loved. Had we advanced this far too quickly? Did we forget the value of the land and how much we depend upon it? Was what happened to one beautiful community destined for all of America? Is it too late for the intelligent application of knowledge and too late to learn from the wisdom of an old Indian?

THE RAILROAD COMES TO HUNTINGTON

First railroad depot, north of tracks and west of New York Avenue, early 1900's.

The town of Huntington Station, originally called Fairground, developed as a result of the Long Island Railroad extending eastward. The first north shore rail line ended at Syosset in 1854, and construction did not resume until 1867. Originally, it was planned to extend the railroad through Cold Spring Harbor and on to Huntington village. The survey was made and actual grading was done just west of St. John's Episcopal Church in Cold Spring Harbor. The original rail bed is now used as the main trail for the present-day nature preserve *(see photo at right)*. In the Town records dated October 12, 1867, the trustees adopted a resolution giving the Long Island Railroad Company a right-of-way over the town property. Apparently a disagreement between the railroad and the landowners resulted in the Long Island Railroad extending the line to the so-called "upper valley" south of the village instead, on the present line to Northport.

Before the railroad, it took *three days* from New York City by stagecoach to the east end of Long Island. At best, it was a tedious trip; imagine three days on a springless horse-drawn stagecoach! The hard-surfaced roads we know today did not exist. The dirt roads were dusty on dry days and muddy on wet days. Both made travel difficult. No doubt many profane words were said over a stuck or broken wagon wheel.

Part of the year I live in Newfane, Vermont, where every March the "mud season" begins. People in Vermont think of this time of the year with the same enthusiasm that we on Long Island have for the coming of a blizzard. There are still many dirt roads in Vermont. The road-beds are raised in the middle, tapering into trenches at the sides to drain and carry off the water. During the mud season, unpaved roads develop deep trenches from the car tires. It becomes possible to line up your tires in these grooves and drive straight ahead without holding onto the steering wheel, like a bumper car in a carnival. These grooves make the roads very hazardous. What difficulty early Long Islanders must have had, riding in horse-drawn stagecoachs over dirt roads!

Irwin Place (still a dirt road in 1922), looking north towards Main Street. Building on corner is the present Town Hall.

When the Long Island Railroad came through, passengers and freight could go from one end of the island to the other in about *five hours*. Although this trip was faster, it was not without its problems. Sparks from the engines would set fire to whole tracts of woodland and residents threatened to tear up the tracks unless something was done to solve the problem. The Long Island Railroad finally screened the locomotives, to the satisfaction of all involved.

In 1867, when passengers arrived at the Huntington Railroad Station, there was nothing but open country north and south of the tracks. The original station house was on-grade, on the north side of the tracks and west of New York Avenue.

By the early 1900's, the only house was north of the station and located midway between Church Street and School Street, just south of where the firehouse would eventually be built. The farm was owned by George Biggs. Just north of the farm was a large pond (appropriately named Biggs Pond), which often spread out onto New York Avenue from rain and melting snow.

Biggs built a hotel on the south end of his land, just north of the railroad station, and named it the North Side Hotel. His son managed it The hotel was never a great success. The last owners were the Mullens family, who changed the name to the Mullens Hotel. In the mid-1930's the hotel was demolished. My father helped a relative of the owner clean out the financial papers, and they found many uncashed checks. Small wonder the hotel went out of business.

The North Side Hotel before 1910. A trolley (right) is arriving with passengers from Halesite and Huntington Village. Railroad tracks can be glimpsed at bottom right.

In 1909-10, New York Avenue was bridged by the railroad and became an underpass. A new station was built on the north side of the tracks, but this time east of New York Avenue, on its present site.

The Long Island Railroad Station was the community's most significant structure, from which our small town eventually took its name. It is the one remaining building that symbolizes the location of Huntington Station. In the wake of destruction around the depot, it is a lasting symbol of the spirit of the kind of people that formed our community.

Rear view of the first railroad depot in Fairground (later Huntington Station), early 1900's. Note cars and electric trolley.

View looking west, with depot just north of tracks. To right of depot is North Side Hotel. At left is Gerlick's Hotel, later the Colonial House.

Another view, probably taken the same day. Building just behind depot at left is Recht and Rosenbaum Pickle Factory. Building at far left is Gerald W. Sweezey Real Estate. A racetrack on Fairground Avenue, one mile south, gave area the name Fairground.

As the creation of Huntington Station is related to the railroad, I inevitably discovered a book entitled *Steel Rails to the Sunrise: The Long Island Railroad,* by Ron Ziel and George Foster — the complete story of one of America's oldest and most unusual railroads. The authors traveled to every town on Long Island to create their pictorial history. Ron has taken over 25,000 photographs of steam engines over the years, traveled to 50 countries, and written 15 books on railroads. Many photos herein are from his collection. Coincidentally, Ron and I both graduated in the R. L. Simpson High School Class of 1957.

LIRR #80 puffing through Huntington Station, 1904; view fron east.

View of New York Avenue in 1910, looking north, while railroad overpass was being built. New train depot was built east of New York Avenue and north of the tracks. Gerlick's Hotel is at right.

View looking north through overpass, October 1918. Note trolley approaching, on its way to Amityville, and North Side Hotel (at left) now above grade.

The new depot, looking east, in 1915. Note trolley in background.

The new depot has undergone some minor changes over the years, but the building with its distinctive curving roof is easily recognizable more than 80 years after it was constructed.

A snowy New Year's Day in 1935, looking west.
The water tower in the background was removed in 1946.

LIRR #50 steaming through the depot in 1952 (looking east).
The signal in front of the building entrance was removed in 1958.

The depot in 1953, the year of Huntington's Tercentenary Celebration (1653-1953).

View from the south side in 1957, just as construction of a new parking area had started. Do you remember the small covered structure on the left?

On August 5, 1950, a serious accident occurred near the Pulaski Road railroad crossing. A locomotive pushing three freight cars (either moving slowly or stopped) was hit by an oncoming passenger train. Forty-six passengers were injured and taken to Huntington Hospital. Apparently the freight brakeman, new to the job, misunderstood the track signals. Both engines had to be scrapped after the accident. This was the last collision between two LIRR steam engines.

Closeup view of collision; note steam still coming from engine.

Railroad workers cleaning up the wreckage. Onlooker in gray suit is Frank Aikman, subsequently the first LIRR president under the MTA.

HUNTINGTON STATION GETS ITS NAME

In the late 1800's, the property about a mile south of the railroad tracks and east of Depot Road (then Fairground Avenue) was converted into a fairground with a one-mile horseracing track. The racetrack was not a big success, but the name Fairground persisted. Years later, when private homes had covered the racetrack area, residents were still finding horseshoes when they planted their gardens.

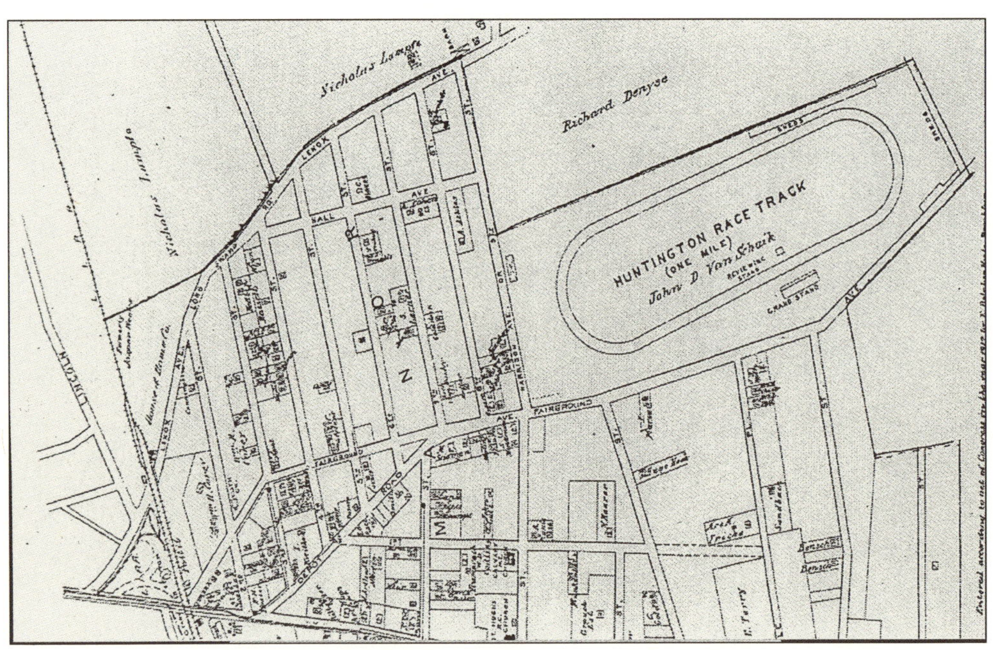

1917 map of Fairground, showing racetrack and adjoining streets.

The fairgrounds in the 1890's. Racetrack is in the foreground.

A. S. Pettit was the first railroad agent, and also became the first postmaster. The post office was established in the railroad station on July 24, 1890 and was called Fairground.

In 1898, Pettit moved the post office to his new place of business near the railroad station, on the west side of New York Avenue. On August 12, 1912, an application was made to change the name of the post office, and with it the name of the growing community became Huntington Station.

Looking south on New York Avenue, about 1900.
The first building on the right was the location of the post office and grocery store owned by A. S. Pettit and his wife Hattie.

Huntington Station about 1912. View looking south on New York Avenue, after overpass was constructed. Note bicycle store on corner of new Pettit Building at right.

Pettit & Sons Coal Lumber & Feed, about 1914. This was the old post office building, minus one chimney. Pettit & Sons eventually merged with six other lumber yards to become Nassau-Suffolk Lumber & Supply.

The Pettit Building in 1920. The storefront once occupied by bicycle shop became the first home of the Huntington Station Bank.

LOCAL TRANSPORTATION

The ability to go quickly from point A to point B is a major reason for our independence today. In three generations, we have progressed from "shank's mare" (my grandmother used to walk to Huntington village and back—sometimes twice a day—with bags of groceries) to horse-drawn vehicles, electric trolleys, gasoline-powered buses, cars and airplanes. A trip from New York to San Francisco by jet is now as commonplace as the stagecoach from Halesite to the Huntington Station depot used to be.

The first street transportation in Huntington was a horse-drawn stage between the harbor in Halesite and the Long Island Railroad depot. "Uncle Jesse" Conklin (1815-1895) drove the stage to and from the depot and carried the mail for 56 years. In all those years he only missed one train, and that was the first time he carried a watch. He never carried the watch again! The photo below shows his "new stage" with up-to-date accessories such as glass windows and back steps.

The stage was eventually replaced by horse-drawn cars which were built and operated by a local company. This route was later taken over by the Long Island

Railroad, which operated it as a trolley line, with power furnished by the Huntington Power and Light Company.

The Halesite trolley depot.

I have been told that mischievous children would often play on the tracks, causing the oncoming trolley to stop. Then one child would climb on top of the trolley and disconnect the power arm, causing a disruption in service and aggravation to the passengers and operator.

Trolley at southwest corner of New York Avenue and Main Street, Huntington, arriving from Huntington Station, 1914.

For a time the trolley line extended service across the Island to Amityville, by way of Farmingdale. However, this extension proved unprofitable and was discontinued. The station-to-harbor service was maintained until 1927, when motor buses took up the work. The streetcar line was first known as the Huntington Railroad Company, then the Huntington Traction Company, and later the Huntington Coach Corporation.

Summer 1914. Written on back: "Left G. Henneborn, conductor, W. Whalters-mgr-adams exp, Henry Wehr, clerk, "Red" Bowden, driver, John Cook, motorman, Hennig, clerk, Oscar Fox, cowcatcher."

As reported in the April 20, 1927 edition of *The Suffolk Bulletin*, a local Huntington newspaper, the Town Board (Supervisor A.L. Field) agreed to allow the Traction Company (Edward T. Dempsey, President) to operate motor buses from Halesite to Huntington Station on New York Avenue. At the same time, the Board canceled the Traction Company's right to maintain a "street railroad" and wanted them to remove all tracks on New York Avenue "except those set in concrete," and to restore the road bed. Mr. Dempsey rejected the proposal on April 27th. This led to weeks of negotiations until a final agreement was reached. It was announced in the August 20, 1927 edition of *The Suffolk Bulletin*. Dempsey received a "20-year franchise" to maintain and operate the motor bus route. He had to have at least four new buses, "each costing not less than $8,000," and the fare in either direction was not allowed to "exceed Ten Cents."

Giving You All the News

THE SUFFOLK BULLETIN

IN SUN RISE LAND

Long Island's North Shore Paper

HUNTINGTON, N. Y., WEDNESDAY, APRIL 20, 1927

VOL. LXXXI No. 9

SUBSCRI

IF WEATHER PERMITS APRIL 24TH WILL SEE FIRST BASEBALL GAME

At Heckscher Park, at Which Time the Season Will Be Officially Opened For This Locality.

By LAURANCE ANGEL, JR.

EXPERIENCE THROUGH COSTLY GENERALLY VERY EFFECTIVE

Transportation Question Nearing Answer; The Town Board Has Tendered a Consent Allowing Running of Busses on N. Y. Ave.

To Huntington Traction Company or to Edw. T. Dempsey, Applicant, Provided Said Traction Company Consents to the Cancellation of the Rights of Said Traction Company to Maintain a Railroad on New York Avenue.

FACTS ARE THE THINGS THAT TELL THE TRUTHFUL STORY

MOSQUITO WORSE THAN CHINESE BANDITS SAYS

Missionary, Who Had to Ride 23 Days on a Pony's Back To Get to Destination.

SEE TO YOUR LIGHTS! IS THE INJUNCTION

Of the Department of Taxa[tion] and Finance Bureau o[f] Motor Vehicles.

COVETED TESTIMONIAL

LEGAL SELF DECEPTION BE-

BLIND BABIES OF N. Y.

The trolley tracks were still visible for years after the service was discontinued and they were covered with blacktop. This 1925 photo of New York Avenue, just south of Main Street in Huntington village, proves the point.

Early motor bus design was an interesting mix of a trolley-like body, a long engine compartment, and a "surrey with the fringe on top." The following photograph from 1927 looks like "Boys Night Out." It was taken at the southwest corner of Main Street and New York Avenue in Huntington village.

Later, buses were enclosed for the comfort of the passengers. This photo, taken at the Halesite Trolley Depot, shows the newer buses as well as two old trolleys then permanently out of service.

By the 1960's, "urban renewal" had begun. Mass transit continued in the Huntington area, with modern buses. The buildings on the east side of New York Avenue in Huntington Station had been destroyed when this photo was taken.

A LOCAL NEWSPAPER

Established in 1847, *The Suffolk Bulletin* began as *The Suffolk Democrat.* Its first editor was Daniel Austin. During the course of my research, I received a book containing all the weekly editions of *The Suffolk Bulletin* for 1927, discovered by Marge Van Velsor Osburn.

I spent many enjoyable weeks reading each issue, in chronological order. Newspapers record events that are *currently happening*, but I read these old issues with the knowledge of what was *going to happen* in the future.

It was an exceptional trip back in time. What was happening in the world in 1927? World War I, the "war to end all wars," had been over for almost nine years, and times were quite good. General Motors announced that it would distribute $2.60 a share, the largest dividend in American history. Babe Ruth hit his 60th home run on September 30. Henry Ford replaced his Model T with the Model A.

It was fascinating to read about the weekly goings-on, with their lack of knowledge that in two short years there would be a stock market collapse on "Black Tuesday"—October 29, 1929. That day of violent trading was the most disastrous in Wall Street history. It was the worst day for total losses, total turnovers, and number of investors ruined. The result would plunge the nation into the Great Depression from which it would take years to recover. In Europe, events were occurring that would eventually cause another world war. Later, a Catholic would become President of the United States. He, his brother and a civil rights leader would be assassinated. Man would travel into space and land on the moon. But back in 1927 their concerns were, of course, only for the present. A thought occurred to me while reading the old issues of *The Suffolk Bulletin*: if we knew the future, what would we do differently now?

In 1927 the paper consisted of four sections: The Suffolk Bulletin (news of Huntington); the Station Times (news of Huntington Station); Northport News (news of Northport); and Kings Park Bulletin (with "all the live items of Kings Park, St. James & Smithtown").

The total number of pages varied from 12 to 18, depending on how much news there was to print. Besides the local news, there was a baseball section, a classified section and advertisements, which they called "Live Wire Notes." It was amusing to see ads of stores I remembered in Huntington Station.

Another section called "Up to the minute news" included all-important facts like:

> "Mrs. S. J. Tilden is recuperating slowly from a recent illness." (2/18)
>
> "The three children of Mr. & Mrs. M. Kunz are all ill with the mumps." (2/18)
>
> "Hollis Meinecke has been on the sick list this week." (8/3)
>
> "Mrs. Margaret Chestnut is having a new roof put on her home on Wyman Avenue." (8/10)
>
> "The heavy rain Monday evening caused damage in many sections. Under the railroad bridge, water was several feet deep and Officer Calver remained on duty, warning autoists of the danger and directing them up Railroad Avenue. Tuesday morning this spot was still impassable." (8/10)

An incident in 1888 shows the "can-do" attitude at *The Suffolk Bulletin.* As the Blizzard of '88 was dumping tons of snow on Huntington, *The Suffolk Bulletin* ran out of paper, and none could be delivered because of the storm. But they managed to get the edition out anyway—printed on wrapping paper supplied by a local merchant. Now that's determination.

If you are interested in reading about the events of 1927, the Huntington Historical Society has copies of *The Suffolk Bulletin.* The Society's library also has a wealth of information in old books, newspapers on microfilm, and photos.

Everything in Readiness

We are now in our new store on New York Avenue with a complete new stock.

Come in and see our new store, visitors welcome.

JAMES FARRELL
Huntington Station
New Phone Number
163

MEAT

THE RIGHT HAND of fellowship is no more sincere than our desire to offer only the choicest cuts of MEATS at prices you usually have to pay for the ordinary kind. The greater pleasure you will have in eating ours would make you very willing to pay more than we ask. Once you taste our meats and poultry you'll not care for any less choice. Let us prove it.

Crystal Market
OTTO DEISEL, Prop.
Prime Meats and Poultry
New York Ave. Tel. Hunt. 1206 Huntington Station

Meinecke's Bread Is Wholesome

Each ingredient in Meinecke's Bread is selected with the utmost care. It must pass a rigid test for purity. It must be fully up to our high standard of quality. Then baked in our sanitary shop, it provides a wholesome food.

Huntington Station Bakery
Hollis Meinecke, Prop.
NEW YORK AVE. HUNTINGTON STATION

My son Rudolph was burned badly around the fingers due to a pot turning over on the stove. We immediately secured a tin of Bernhard's All Healing Ointment and put this ointment all over burns. It surely was a blessing as in the course of a week the fingers were entirely healed and today there is no trace of any scars. It should be in every home for emergencies of this kind.

Signed,
MRS. ACOMPORA.
Depot Road, Huntington Station.

BERNHARD'S DRUG STORE
New York Ave. Opp. Post Office
HUNTINGTON STATION

NOTICE! The Lunch Wagon at the Station is open for business! Pure food at reasonable prices. Ladies' patronage solicited.
New York Ave. at May Street G. H. Reeves, Prop.

Wiggin's Garage

Get Your Car Ready for Spring!

DEPENDABLE AUTO REPAIRING

Taxi, Baggage and Express Service
Corner N. Y. Ave. & Nassau Ave.
HUNTINGTON STATION, L. I.
Tel. 611

ANNOUNCING THE OPENING OF

Huntington's Newest General Store

— on —
SATURDAY, MARCH 19th
— at —
335 New York Avenue

OFFERING TO THE PUBLIC COMPLETE AND UP-TO-DATE LINES OF
ARMY AND NAVY GOODS
WORK CLOTHES
SPORTS WEAR
CAMP EQUIPMENT
GENT'S FURNISHINGS
SHOES and
GENERAL DRY GOODS

SPECIAL OPENING DAY PRICES ON ALL MERCHANDISE

It is our aim and desire to serve with reliable and quality merchandise at a great saving to you.
Come in and convince yourself by inspecting our new store, whether or not you intend to purchase.
We have many useful items on our display counters, some of which you may be looking for.
Useful souvenirs given to every purchaser.

H. MARSH
335 New York Avenue Huntington, N. Y.
(Just Above Main Street)

Advertisements in The Suffolk Bulletin *provide a window into Huntington Station life in the late 1920's.*

BUSINESSES DEVELOP IN HUNTINGTON STATION

With the new railroad providing virtually weather-proof service, businesses close to Huntington Harbor relocated to the Huntington Station area. One of these businesses was Huntington Lumber & Coal Co., shown below in early photos.

Huntington Lumber & Coal Co., 1912. Note harbor at right. This building also served as the Halesite Post Office.

Huntington Lumber & Coal in the 1920's, after relocation to the southeast corner of Second Street and New York Avenue.

Over the years new businesses came to Huntington Station, and the community began to flourish. An early arrival to the Station area was Concannon's, shown below in a photo from 1935.

FREDDIE'S SHOE REPAIR, 1157 NEW YORK AVENUE

Alfred A. Sforza, affectionately known as *Freddie the shoemaker,* recently celebrated his 62nd year in business in the Town of Huntington. Fred took over his brother-in-law Mike Aurricchio's shoe repair business in Huntington Station on March 3, 1934, when Mike Aurricchio died.

Looking southwest on New York Avenue, 1910. The two small stores next to the North Side Hotel were the barber shop and Mike Aurricchio Shoe Repair.

Fred has always been known as an "easy hit." Children coming into town without money could ask Freddie to borrow a dime for candy or ice cream. Emma (Jackson) Gumbs said that she probably owes Freddie $1,000 from all the dimes she "borrowed." The elderly, if they stopped to rest in a chair in his store, would be assured of him rushing out to buy them a soda or ice cream bar. When any of his customers met with hard times, they'd often hear his gravelly, rough voice say "no charge." And no insisting would change his mind.

Mike Aurricchio in his shop, 1920's.

Throughout the years, Fred's shop has served as a meeting place to discuss current events. Mornings are still reserved for coffee and rolls and arguing local and national politics. During World War II, his storefront window displayed a large number of pictures sent to him by Huntington serviceman overseas. Men on leave from the war stopped by at Freddie's to find out if others had made it back home. Although many of these photos have faded, some still remain in his collection.

Freddie's Shoe Repair, 1940's. From left to right: Nate Sandella, Chris "Knock" Stubbolo, Fred Sforza, Charlie Aurricchio.

He met Lena Bifulco, who would later become his wife, when she brought in a pocketbook to be repaired. They were married November 29, 1936. He maintains that since then "she has been fixin' *my* pocketbook."

They have a son, Dr. Alfred V. Sforza (his wife is Barbara), three grandchildren, Dr. Anthony V. Sforza (his wife is Elizabeth), Debra Sforza Smith, (her husband is Peter E. Smith, a local architect) and Sharon Sforza. They also have four great-grandchildren, Kevin Sforza, Kyle Sforza, Jessica Smith and Nicholas Smith.

When urban renewal demolished many of the stores in the little community of Huntington Station, Fred, the "unofficial mayor," moved his store in 1965 to its present site at 308 New York Avenue in Huntington village, where he is still dedicated to his shoe repair business. On May 29, 1994 a plaque was placed on the building, honoring his contribution to the town of Huntington. Town Supervisor Frank Petrone declared May 29th as Fred Sforza Day, honoring his contribution to Huntington history.

Joe's Barber Shop, 1151 New York Avenue

This store had a dome-like entrance with windows on either side. In each section, Joe had children's barber seats. One seat was a horse, and the other was an automobile. You had a choice as to which one to sit in to have your hair cut—a difficult decision for a child to make. You knew you were becoming a "big boy" when Joe would get out the booster seat so you could sit in the adult chair.

Jacobson's Pharmacy, 1 Broadway

The original site, in the early 20's, was occupied by Cuttings' Pharmacy. Cuttings joined with another pharmacist to form Cuttings & Kassel. The two eventually went their own ways; Cuttings moved to Huntington village while Kassel stayed and the store became known as the Huntington Station Pharmacy.

At the time, before a pharmacist could be certified after graduation, he had to have two years' experience. The Huntington Station Pharmacy served as a launching pad for other pharmacies. Some other pharmacists who apprenticed at this store were Irving Shear (who then opened his own pharmacy on New York Avenue and 11th Street) and Sam Kline (who opened in Kings Park).

Harold Jacobson's father was born in England and moved to Brooklyn. His plumbing business took him on many trips to Long Island, where he eventually settled. Harold was born in 1915 to Barnett and Esther Jacobson in Copiague and soon after moved to Amityville. Harold graduated from St. John's University in 1936—the first year they granted a Bachelor of Science in Pharmacy degree. The summer after graduation he worked with a classmate in a drug store in Fleishman, New York. It was there that he met Frances Eagol, whom he eventually married.

In September 1936, Harold began his apprenticeship at an East Northport drug store. During this time he found out that Mr. Kassel was seriously ill and his drug store was for sale. The store was in disrepair, but Harold looked beyond the dust and spider webs and saw a beautiful tile floor, a marble ice cream soda fountain, glass top tables, glass display cabinets, sliding ladders to reach all shelves and a potential to make it a better pharmacy. He and Fran worked many hours cleaning and doing all the repairs themselves. Harold's hours kept him busy from 7:30 a.m. to midnight, seven days a week. He even moved closer to the store so he could walk to work in case of a snowstorm or an emergency.

His success was based not only on keeping long hours, but on his being known as a kind and considerate person. Up to his retirement, he enjoyed being a part of the many generations of Huntington Station families.

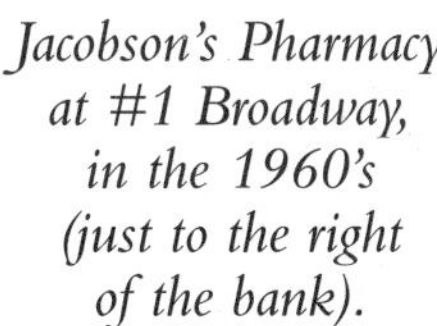

Jacobson's Pharmacy at #1 Broadway, in the 1960's (just to the right of the bank).

During our interview, Harold told me that when he came to Huntington Station in 1941, the use of leeches for bloodletting was still recommended occasionally by older physicians. He had a leech supplier in Long Island City called Yacobelli's.

Leech is the common name for more than 300 types of annelid worms. They range in size from less than an inch to 12 inches long. Most leeches live in ponds and streams, where they feed on worms, snails, or attach themselves to a wading bird or an unsuspecting human. A tubelike structure is then forced into the tissue of the victim, and three knifelike jaws slice through the skin. The wound is anesthetized by an as-yet-unknown substance. The saliva of leeches contains an anticoagulant (hirudin) which prevents and dissolves blood clots. Researchers are investigating the usefulness of proteins in this saliva for treating cardiovascular disease. Medicinal leeches were once widely used for bloodletting. They are still employed by surgeons to maintain circulation in small blood vessels during delicate operations.

Harold told me that many ethnic groups had other ways of bloodletting. One was to put a match under an inverted glass. This created a vacuum, so that when the glass was placed over the skin it acted like a suction cup, causing the skin to rise and blood to "suck out." (A scene from the movie "Godfather II" shows this procedure being performed on the Godfather's baby son.)

Harold and I moved on to a discussion of urban renewal. He said as early as 1941, the State was threatening to take down all the buildings in Huntington Station. "The fear of urban renewal kept everyone from updating their stores and buildings," he asserted. I noticed that this fear was consistent in almost all of the interviews I had with business owners. The "black cloud" of threatened urban renewal was the reason improvements to storefronts and businesses were not made. Owners and renters were not willing to put improvements into buildings that could be destroyed at any time. The deterioration that inevitably followed the threat of urban renewal just added more fuel to the fire. It gave the proponents of urban renewal more reason to continue their quest to "revitalize" Huntington Station. I have had a gnawing feeling since starting to write the story of our community that this total destruction could have been avoided if incentives had been given to the businesses, by the Town or the State, to do their *own* improvements. What incentive do you have to improve your property when improvements are penalized by higher taxes? Governments always need more tax money, because they have no incentive to live within a budget — a never-ending spiral. I think the phrase is "Catch-22."

Scalzo Oil, 13 School Street

Nick LoScalzo was born in Manhattan in 1906. His family operated an ice business in Manhattan, where Nick worked until 1925, when he started his own ice business in Huntington Station with Jim Nicholetti (Nick Bros.) opposite St. Hugh's Church. In 1933, at a wedding in Brooklyn, he met D. Maria Digilio, affectionately known as "Dolly." By coincidence, the LoScalzo and Digilio families came from the same town in Italy. Her family also owned and operated an ice and coal business in Brooklyn. They were married in 1935 and had three children, Corbina, John, and Patricia.

From 1925 to 1940, Nick operated his business on New York Avenue opposite St. Hugh's. From 1940 to 1945 he sold ice, coal and wood from a small building on New York Avenue just north of School Street. Most old timers remember this 10x10 cinder block building. Nick would pick up ice at Huntington Ice & Cube on Steward Avenue in Huntington, and deliver to all his customers. The small ice house in Huntington Station made it convenient for local pickups. In 1945, he moved his business to 13 School Street. During the 1950's, his brother Rocky delivered ice cubes to restaurants and catering halls. Cake ice sold for a penny a pound, delivered.

In recent times, exercise has been known to contribute to good physical health in later life. Observing how well Nick looks today, I wondered how much genetics played a part and how much the physical exercise helped. He remembers carrying huge blocks of ice, wrapped in burlap bags, to stores in Huntington

Station, and sometimes delivering to the second floor of homes. When I asked about his physical ability to do this kind of work, his first comment was that he used to "get wet a lot." I'll bet he was in great shape.

Nick also sold kerosene for homes that didn't have central heating and used space heaters. Coal was also used to heat homes, and originally came into Huntington by way of the harbor. When the railroad came through in 1867, it was more convenient and reliable to pick up coal kept in side cars by the railroad depot. Coal was eventually replaced by oil for heating homes.

During World War II, Nick received an oil allocation based on use and the ration stamps from his customers. He would pick up oil from tanks in Huntington Harbor owned by Mr. Pettit. Most of his oil came from Long Island Ice in Riverhead, operated by the Conklin family.

Urban renewal forced him to relocate in 1968 to his present site at 115 West 11th Street. Nick and Dolly still show up at work almost every day. The business is now operated by his son John, and grandchildren—a true family business, and one of the best examples of the types of families we had in our community. John, in addition to running a business, has found time to be a volunteer fire fighter (Huntington Fire Department), Fire Chief, and Fire Commissioner.

One of the advantages in growing up in a small town is that you know people for such a long time, you almost forget whether they are friends or relatives. John and I started elementary school together and were in the same class right through high school, along with a whole crew of boys and girls. The following photograph was taken in 1947, overlooking the Roosevelt School playground. Most of the students pictured here graduated from high school together.

Second grade class, Roosevelt Elementary School, 1947. John LoScalzo is in the front row, third from right, with the author directly behind him.

M. A. Connell Funeral Home, 934 New York Avenue

Michael A. Connell opened the first undertaker's parlor in Huntington Station in 1923. In those days the idea of a "funeral home" was practically unheard of. The undertaker's parlor was simply a display room where caskets were shown for selection. Wakes were customarily held in the family home of the deceased. Mike's first place of business was at 971 New York Avenue, next to the Gordon-Kerner Produce building.

Connell home, built in 1931. Extension on right was first funeral parlor in Huntington Station.

The Connell family had come to the United States in the 1840's. Grandfather Connell later built a home at 44 Maple Hill Road in Huntington. Mike would play his trumpet in the back yard, serenading the nurses in their quarters alongside Huntington Hospital. One nurse, Florence McIntyre, was impressed with the young man; they began courting, and married in 1930.

By the 1930's, having a funeral director provide all the services for the family of the deceased in the privacy of a funeral home became the more common practice. Mike built the funeral home at its present location in 1931. In the beginning, funeral homes were open from 11:00 a.m. to 11:00 p.m., to serve people who were used to long, extended funerals at home.

M.A. Connell Funeral Home, 1995

In 1956, major renovations and expansions began, and continued until the building looked the way it appears now. Today, Mike's children and grandchildren are continuing the business — another example of the Huntington Station tradition of family enterprises.

A. L. JACOBSEN FUNERAL HOME, 1380 NEW YORK AVENUE

A. L. Jacobsen Funeral Home was founded in 1928 by Alfred and Grace Jacobsen, just north of the present location on the corner of New York Avenue and Pulaski Road next to Flowerdale Florist. They moved to the present site in 1932. Today, the funeral home is owned and operated by Christian Jacobsen and his sister Karen Jacobsen Bosak.

A.L. Jacobsen Funeral Home, 1920's.

This is a business that survived the ravages of urban renewal, which was to start north of the railroad tracks and proceed south to Jericho Turnpike. The purpose was to revitalize the are's residential and commercial properties. The owners were supposed to receive the right of first refusal on the new structures. The State bought up properties, destroyed the structures but never rebuilt the area.

Chris Jacobsen remembers the State keeping many of these properties on the "chopping block," even though nothing was done. As late as 1971, the state still had properties that it was going to "revitalize." You couldn't improve, sell, or lease for fear of the State taking the property. "Urban renewal was the virus that caused the decay of the area," Chris said. It wasn't until they removed these prop-

A.L. Jacobsen Funeral Home, 1995.
Note upper part of original building, at right.

erties from the maps that improvements started, not by the State, but by the private owners.

Karen has many early memories of Huntington Station. There was a feed store across the street, on the corner of Pulaski Road (then called 7th Avenue) and New York Avenue, that sold live rabbits painted pink and yellow, at Easter time. Every year Lincoln Elementary School had a contest on the playgroundfor the best or most unusual pets, with blue ribbons given; Chris said that the Schwab family always seemed to win with their horses.

Chris remembers the Boy Scouts camping out behind Kerber's Egg Farm on Pulaski Road, and the milkman and breadman selling tiny loaves of bread with comic books for children. He recalls fireworks at Manor Field and motor boat races in Huntington Harbor. But one of his most vivid recollections is of a whale. On October 21, 1946, a 63-foot finback whale entered Huntington Harbor and beached itself off Halesite Park. The next day, the schools were let out and people came from miles around to witness the last hours of the great sea mammal.

Dying whale in Huntington Harbor, October 22, 1946.

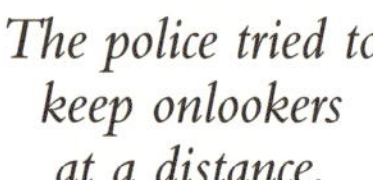

The police tried to keep onlookers at a distance.

DIAMOND'S DEPARTMENT STORE, 1203 NEW YORK AVENUE

Leonard Diamond's grandfather, Isaac Levenbron, was born in Austria and came to New York in the early 1900's. He later moved to Huntington Station and opened a general store near Sarrow's. Leonard's father Isador Diamond lived in Lindenhurst. He traveled by trolley car from Lindenhurst to Huntington Station to court Bertha Levenbron. In 1923, they married and had two children, Leonard and Burdge. In 1924, they opened Diamond's, on the west side of New York Avenue, north of the tracks. Before the Great Depression of the 1930's they sold very fine men's wear, but after the Depression started, no one had the money to spend on expensive suits. To change with the times, they introduced general clothing for men, women and children, and shoes and work clothes. In those days women's dresses sold for 98 cents, and men's suits were $22.50.

After urban renewal, Diamond Work Clothes Center moved to 344 New York Avenue in Huntington village. For the next 18 years until retirement, they sold outdoor clothes, hiking boots, gloves, winter wear, and sport shirts.

View of Diamond's on New York Avenue from the "cop's booth," early 1950s. Police officer is Sam Macedonia.

"We enjoyed the years in the village," Leonard told me, "but we often think of our wonderful beginnings in Huntington Station.

"The railroad station was clean and pretty, with beautiful flowers planted all around. Huntington Station was a really close, family oriented community. I remember people being very nice. They came in not only to buy things, but also for conversation. I noted in later years in the village, people did not engage in much conversation.

"Huntington Station was always treated like a stepchild by the Huntington town fathers. The Station died a horrible death, almost like a cancer. Small areas at a time were allowed to deteriorate, until the whole town was gone."

During our conversation, Leonard spoke mostly of the items he sold and the people he met. He never even hinted at how generous he and his family were to the residents of Huntington Station; countless times he supplied clothing for the poor people in the area. Leonard Diamond exemplifies the spirit of the business people who were part of old Huntington Station.

Same view as in photograph on page 45, after urban renewal. Most occupants had already moved or just closed their businesses.

CLARENDON INN, 1201 NEW YORK AVENUE

Fred Ulmer, co-owner of the Clarendon Inn from 1928 to 1946, was born in Brooklyn in 1903. His uncle had a summer place on 23rd Street in Huntington Station, and while Fred was growing up he often visited him.

While at a dance at the Brooklyn Labor Lyceum, Fred met Annabelle Bosch; they married in 1927 and moved to Huntington Station. The following year Fred, along with Oscar Pause, started the Clarendon Inn — a bar and grill which served a businessmen's lunch and specialized in German food.

As early as 1941, the threat of urban renewal began to loom over the business owners in Huntington Station. By 1946, Fred and Oscar decided to sell the business. Fred owned the building and wanted to keep it, but it was threatened with condemnation and he had to sell. As shown in the photo above, the sign was still there after urban renewal, when the Inner Circle occupied the building.

The Clarendon Inn in 1935.

Interior view, 1935. The owner, Fred Ulmer, is behind the bar, in the foreground.

LAMBERTA HARDWARE, 160 DEPOT ROAD

Charles Lamberta was the original owner of Lamberta Hardware. The store was built in 1951. There are many stories about the generosity and sense of community that this man gave to Huntington Station. One episode is remembered by Florence Bowes, a teacher at Toaz Junior High School in Huntington Station:

"Mr. Lamberta of Lamberta's Hardware brought gleams of joy to youngsters who never received toys or presents of any kind. Witness the day I brought a sad-looking two wheeler bike, salvaged from someone's garbage, to his store. The bike was slightly lopsided, missing one pedal and the chain. With an innocent look I said, 'Can you fix it?' He studied the mess for a moment and said optimistically, 'I'll try. Come back in a couple of days and we'll see.'

"Two days later I returned to find a freshly painted bike with a new chain and two new matching pedals just begging for the company of some wanting youngster. When I asked what I owed him, Mr. Lamberta smiled and said, 'Just let me see the look on the kid's face when he gets the bike.' A happy and thankful boy and this Station man eventually met. After that, toy trucks with no wheels in need of paint and fixing became part of Lamberta's life. Charles Lamberta, giver of joy and happiness to others, epitomized what it was to be a Huntington Station man."

Charlie was also a Brooklyn Dodger fan. In those days, you had to be truly devoted to root for the Brooklyn Dodgers. This was because prior to 1955, and for as long as I can remember, Brooklyn always played the Yankees in the World Series and Brooklyn always lost. Sticking by a losing team was the test of a true fan.

Charlie's daughter, Laurette Lamberta Prisco, remembers the abuse all Brooklyn Dodger fans took in those early years, and Charlie was no exception.

"When Brooklyn defeated the Yankees in 1955," she told me, "it was time for my father to get back at all his neighbors. First he made a large dummy of a Yankee player and hung it from his front porch. Multicolored balloons were everywhere. He set up a public address system with large speakers and waited for his Yankee neighbors to return home from work. One by one he announced their names over the loudspeaker and said that if they crawled up to his house on their hands and knees with their heads bowed, they could have a drink with him. Everyone, with just a little resentment, happily participated in his little prank.

"Mom was taking movies of the whole episode. Dad was so happy to have a drink with these very embarrassed Yankee fans. I'll remember this as long as I live."

Mohlenhoff's Greenhouse and Flower Shop

John and Marie Mohlenhoff owned and operated a farm in St. Albans, Queens. In the 1930's a major highway was built that separated their farm house from their fields. Getting access to their fields became difficult. John and Marie decided to move their farm, and came to Huntington in July 1937. The greenhouse in front, at their present location, was the original greenhouse from the farm in St. Albans, and was transported to Huntington.

John Mohlenhoff Sr. and "Charley Horse" in the greenhouse, 1938.

The conditions in the Mohlenhoff's new home were spartan at best. The house was in disrepair and many of the windows were broken. They often shot bats at dusk. The whole family smiled when telling me about Mike Seminara, a family friend who came out from St. Albans to help repair the house. Every night Mike would sleep with a stocking over his head, for fear of bats.

John was the flower grower and originally only sold flowers wholesale. Occasionally, Marie would make up a bouquet for some local residents. Early in the 1940's, Marie attended a floral design school in New York City, and the growing/retail flower business of Mohlenhoff's was started. Today, the business is operated by their son, Jack Mohlenhoff, his wife Marylou, and their sons, John and Michael.

Jack remembers this area as having many small farms. As children, they played polo in the fields off Jericho Turnpike. "Polo," he reflected a few seconds, and said, "Actually, all we had was the horses and broomsticks." Sometimes they would go out onto Jericho Turnpike to retrieve a lost ball and "there was hardly any traffic at all." Jericho Turnpike had potato fields with "rows of plantings right up to the edge of the road." Although his home was heated, the bedrooms were usually cold—cold enough sometimes to freeze the contents of a chamber pot. (We have so many conveniences today; it's hard to remember that it wasn't always this way.)

During World War II, Jack remembers how our boys, before leaving for the war, would stop off and give Marie a list of dates (birthdays etc.), to send flowers while they were away. Marylou remembers the Mohlenhoffs receiving telegrams from our servicemen in foreign countries, requesting flowers to be sent to a loved one. Those who did return paid her when they came back home. But Jack told me that if she didn't get paid, "she wouldn't have cared."

Actually, Jack and Marylou represent two businesses in our little town. Marylou's father, Lou Maas, owned and operated the Royal Scarlet Quality Market with Robert Maas and Nicholas Schwartz. The shop was located on 1171 New York Avenue Marylou remembers being in her father's store collecting ration stamps and grease during the war. "Huntington Station was very active in the war effort," she said. Marylou also remembered the "double features"at the Huntington Station Movie Theater. In between the two features they would sell bonds for the war effort. Children, who of course did not have the $7.50, $18.75 or $37.50 to buy a bond, were encouraged to do their part by buying stamps at 20 or 50 cents, to fill a book of stamps. When the book was completed the child could buy a bond, to the tune of "Buy, Buy a Bond."

The Mohlenhoff family: From top, Marylou and Jack, Michael, Marie and John.

In the 1950's, the Maases left the Quality Market business and operated the Superior Grill at Jericho Turnpike and New York Avenue. Then the the State threatened to build a cloverleaf at the intersection. This caused the demise of their business, and of course the State never built the cloverleaf.

At the end of this interview, Marylou, with tears in her eyes, remembered the year (1989) her mother died. Mrs. Maas had left a letter detailing the articles she wished to give each of her children; she also wrote that she was thankful for her life, her children and her country. I thought about how proud I was to know this family and all our families in our community.

Huntington Station Theater, 1131 New York Avenue

People have fond memories of going to the movies in this small theater, but the only photographs I found show the theater secondary to events like parades. In the photo below, the theater marquee is just to the right of center.

The photo below was taken after urban renewal caused the demise of many businesses. One-half of the first building on the left had been the theater; the other half had been occupied by Mattie's, a stationery and ice cream store.

In the 1940's, movies were a great part of everyone's lives. The stars were bigger than life, and we all had our heros. Saturday matinees were usually reserved for children and they often showed westerns. Cowboy movies were always filled with action, comedy and songs. The words of the songs used to tell America to do the right thing. I doubt if the younger generation can fully appreciate the excitement generated by a Saturday afternoon cowboy movie at the Huntington Station Theater. I can still hear the cheers of the children in the audience as the cavalry, with the bugler blasting *charge* on his horn, came to the rescue of the wagon train.

The good guy was always a handsome clean-cut cowboy, riding a white stallion. He always had a sidekick. The good guy could ride a horse, play his guitar and shoot at the same time. His pistol never ran out of bullets. When he shot the bad guy, we never saw any blood. Sometimes he was such a great marksman that he could shoot the gun right out of the bad guy's hand, without risking life or limb.

The movie cowboy back then had his own code of conduct. He was always on the side of good, never mean to anyone, the champion of the underdog, and used his powers to fight prejudice and the forces of nature. He had great leadership abilities to pull everyone together for the common good. He always had the time to help a troubled kid, or to teach a kid how to handle hard times. What a great, all-around guy. No wonder we left the movies feeling good.

When Federal laws changed how the movie studios controlled their stars, and forced them to sell their theater chains, the movie industry began to change. It no longer played such a major role in American life. Weekly attendance began to drop, from 80 million in the 1940's to 12 million in the 1970's. Television was the straw that broke the camel's back, taking much of the audience away from movie theaters.

In front of ticket booth at Huntington Station Theater in the 1940's: from left, Frank Court, Jeanette Sammis and Bill Nolan.

HUNTINGTON STATION BANK, 1168-1170 NEW YORK AVENUE

On Friday evening, August 6, 1920, a meeting was held in the offices of Koster & Cornehlsen, in Huntington Station. This was the first meeting of the incorporators of the Huntington Station Bank. The following are the first three pages of the minutes and bylaws book of the newly formed bank, dated August 6, 1920. Note that the pages are handwritten.

1

Minutes of First Meeting of Incorporators of Huntington Station Bank.

The first meeting of the incorporators and subscribers to the capital stock of the Huntington Station Bank, was held at the office of Koster and Cornehlsen at Huntington Station, N.Y. on Friday Evening, August 6th, 1920 at 8:00 o'clock.

Mr. Frederick H. Koster called the meeting to order and stated the purposes thereof.

Upon motion, Mr. Frederick H. Koster was chosen chairman of the meeting, and Mr. Samuel T. Cheshire Secretary thereof.

On calling roll of stockholders, consisting of the following named gentlemen

Frederick H. Koster Victor Bruns
Christ Cornehlsen Floyd G. Baylis
Isak Lewenbron Samuel T. Cheshire
Stanley E. Pettit Theodore S. Hall
Hugh P. Arthur Isaac R. Swezey
Francis X. Wunsch

the following with the number of shares subscribed by each of them were found to be present:

Name	Shares Subscribed
Frederick H. Koster	23
Chris Cornehlsen	23
Stanley E. Pettit	23
Victor Bruns	23
Floyd E. Baylis	23
Samuel T. Cheshire	22
Theodore G. Hall	22
Isaac R. Swezey	22
	181

The chairman thereupon stated that a notice of this meeting had been given to all subscribers to the capital stock, whereupon, on motion, a copy of said notice was ordered placed on file.

The chairman then stated that the organization certificate had been filed in the office of the Banking Department of the State of New York at Albany, N.Y. on the 3rd day of August, 1920, and duly approved by the Superintendent of Banks, and a certified copy thereof, duly filed in the County Clerk's Office of Suffolk County on the 5th day of August, 1920.

The chairman submitted for the consideration of the meeting the proposed by-laws and stated that the same had been prepared by the counsel of

3

the Bank in accordance with the instructions of the incorporators.

After discussion and consideration, and by unanimous vote, it was

Resolved, that the by-laws now submitted to this meeting be, and hereby are adopted as the by-laws of the corporation, and that said by-laws be prefixed to the minutes of this meeting.

There being no other business before the meeting, it was adjourned.

Samuel T. Cheshire
Secretary

Fred H Koster
Chairman

The book is part of the bank memorabilia collection of Ray Devine, a former vice president of the bank.

The first officers of the bank were: Fred H, Koster, President; Stanley Pettit, Vice-President; Theodore S. Hall, Vice-President; Samuel T. Cheshire, Cashier, and Paul E. Shaefer, Assistant Cashier.

Ray Devine and his family came to the Huntington Station area from Bay Ridge, Brooklyn in April 1936. Ray attended the South Huntington Schools. His banking career was spent in the Huntington Station area; he joined the Huntington Station Bank in 1951 as a bookkeeper, advancing to a teller, officer and subsequently retiring as a Vice President at NatWest Bank.

First building on right is the original Huntington Station Bank, 1920.

"The Huntington Station Bank was truly a small town bank," Ray recalled. "Most people in the community knew each other and used our bank. They particularly enjoyed being known on a personal basis by the employees and officers.

"The Huntington Station Bank offered business and personal checking, savings accounts, home mortgages, short-term business loans, home improvement loans and auto loans. Most of the auto loans were for the purchase of used cars; at the time, few people could afford the luxury of a new car.

"Loans were practically on a handshake; the lending officer and customer usually knew each other. Documentation was very minimal. Today, regulations imposed by governmental agencies make for an abundance of documentation even for the smallest of loans.

"Customers relished the idea of having a personal contact within the bank. It made them at ease in filling their needs. Today, computers have arrived on the banking scene, leaving very few personable and knowledgeable individuals to tend to the needs of the community. The customers, who once enjoyed personal contact with a teller or bank officer, are often directed to an ATM or touch tone telephone, where they may not be able to get answers to their questions. If they don't use the new automated systems, they must endure long lines at the teller stations because fewer employees are at hand. Some banks are even imposing a service fee if one asks to approach a teller window.

"It's understandable that most customers are finding it difficult to handle even the smallest banking transaction. The days of professional service are fast becoming a memory of yesterday's banks."

The Huntington Station Bank opened September 10, 1920. On that day, the newly established bank announced that the first day's deposits were over $75,000.00 from 60 depositors. By 1952, the bank served more than 11,000 depositors and had a total of $9,500,000.00 in deposits and loans.

The Huntington Station Bank in the 1930's, on the northeast corner of Broadway and New York Avenue.

Eventually, larger banks took over small town banks and banking became more global than local. In 1957 the Huntington Station Bank became the Bank of Huntington. In the early 1960's the Bank of Huntington became the Meadowbrook National Bank and then the National Bank of North America. In 1968, NatWest Bank took it over. Ray remembers the day they moved the bank to 9th Street and New York Avenue. The site had been the former home of Dr. Milstein, a Huntington Station dentist. On that day, sections of safety deposit boxes were picked up by a fork lift and placed on a flatbed truck. Three men with shotguns protected the move. This branch is closing soon, and future banking will be carried on in their other branches.

The Huntington Station Bank's motto was "The Bank of Complete and Friendly Service." Friendly it certainly was, and complete as well. Ray and his peers were taught by seasoned bankers who served each customer in a professional manner, and with wisdom and compassion.

There were many other businesses in Huntington Station before urban renewal; the following is a partial list which should bring back memories of the days when our shopping community was still intact:

Recht & Rosenbaum Pickle &
  Kraut Factory
LaPera Bar & Grill
Wehr's Grocery
Gerlick's Restaurant
  later, Colonial House
North Side Hotel
  later, Mullen's Hotel
  then Larkhart Lincoln/Mercury
Boyle's Diner
Rotella, tailor
A. S. Pettit & Sons
  later, Nassau Suffolk Lumber
Fusaro's Shoe Repair
DiSpirito's Meat Market
Charlie's Barber Shop
Reese's Ice Cream
  later, Joost's Ice Cream
Hulsen/Maggi Stationery
  later, Popkin's
Silberfein Dress Factory
Horne Paint
  later, Lesne Law Office
Dave's Stationery
Hollis's Bakery
Levy Fruit Store
  later, Carino Fruit Store
A & P
Axelrod's Clothing
Ben Franklin 5 & 10
Schleffler Real Estate
Wohl's Drugs
Elsie's Deli
Barnett Children Clothes
Cromwell's Sweet Shop
Liberty Diner
Cooper's Clothing
Fehlheison Stationery
Schultz Children Clothes
Joe's Barber Shop
Interstate Furniture
Jet's
Nat's Men's Clothing
Jewelers, John Theofel
Beauty Parlor
Mattie's
Deboe's Bicycle
Chinese Laundry (Rbt. Young)
Aida Bar
Aronson's
  later, Ponsies Barber Shop
Adelman's
Huntington Plumbing
Gordon's Children Clothes
Shaiken Deli
Aronson's Furniture
Raskin Bros.
Spampanto's Shoe Repair
  (two brothers, two stores)
James Butler
Penn Furniture
Friedman & Haas Furniture
Rubin's Cleaners & Tailor
Levenbron Dry Goods
Louis Fruit & Vegetable
Sarrow's
Auto Glass
Applebaum Dress Factory
Nat's Work Clothes
A. B. Gross Auto Accessories
Halpern Stationery
North Shore Paper Co.
Paramount Glass
Brown's Deli
Gordon & Kerner Produce
Teich Dairy
Kingsland & Kaufman Gas
Herman's Butcher

Levy's Butcher
Dixie Belle Bar
Mascaro's Bar
Smitty's Gas
Cozy Corner Restaurant
Gatto's Music
DeRosa's Fish Store
Holbreich Liquor
Harwein Hardware
Farrell's
Walsdorf Insurance
Freedman Jewelers
Raskin & Haas, Esqs.
Crystal Market
August, Barber
Safaelo's Restaurant
Campus Restaurant
Wuest Deli
Semon Insurance & Real Estate
Gold Insurance
Romano's Bakery
Weber's Garage
later, Recreation (Billiard Hall)
Porco's Tavern
Lukralle Furniture
Price's Bakery
Steuben Bar & Grill
Kanter & Levenberg, accountants
Jones' Candy
Costa's Candy
Wiggins' Garage

After urban renewal destroyed the area, some businesses relocated elsewhere in Huntington. A few are still in the same place. Most disappeared, and the places where they used to thrive became just a parking lot. Some of the survivors are:

Freddie's Shoe Repair
1157 New York Avenue, moved to 308 New York Avenue, Huntington
Walsdorf Insurance
1140 New York Avenue, moved to 770 New York Avenue
Freedman Jewelers
1140 New York Avenue, moved to 345 New York Avenue, Huntington
Jacobson's Pharmacy (now retired)
1 Broadway, moved to the Big H
Raskin & Haas
1146 New York Avenue, moved to 34 Dewey Street, Huntington
Scalzo Fuel Oil
13 School Street, moved to 115 West 11th Street, Huntington Station
Huntington Station Jewelers
1155 New York Avenue, 5 Broadway, moved to the Big H
Diamond's Department Store
(now retired)
1203 New York Avenue, moved to 344 New York Avenue, Huntington
Lukralle Bros. Furniture
(now Huntington Van & Storage)
31 Broadway, moved to 94 Elm Street, Huntington
Lamberta Hardware
160 Depot Road, Huntington Station
Porco's Tavern
(now Chapman's)
25 Broadway, Huntington Station

COMMUNITY SERVICES

HUNTINGTON MANOR FIRE DEPARTMENT

In the United States, over *two million* fires occur each year, causing thousands of deaths and injuries and billions of dollars in property damage. Until the mid-18th century, towns had only the fire watchman and the volunteer bucket brigades to fight fires. The bucket brigades were volunteers wheeling, (by hand or using horses) wooden tubs filled with water to the site of the fire. They passed water buckets to each other in a line. Later they used hand-operated pumps. To be effective, the fire fighters had to work close to the fire, and were often burned themselves. By the turn of the 20th century, the internal combustion engine began to replace horse-drawn, hand-operated pumps and was able to generate enough water to fight large fires.

Early 20th century firefighting equipment.

Everyone is aware of the many careers of Benjamin Franklin as printer, inventor, scientist, statesman and philosopher, but few know that he organized the first permanent fire company in 1736 in Philadelphia. Today, nearly every community is served by an organized fire department. Of the one million fire fighters in the United States, 250,000 are full-time career professionals. The remainder are either paid for each alarm they answer or are volunteers who receive no pay. The 23,000 all-volunteer fire departments serve about 25% of the population. Firefighting is an extremely hazardous occupation. More praise should be given to the men of our community who voluntarily put their lives on the line to protect us.

The oldest volunteer fire department on Long Island is in Sag Harbor; it was formed in 1803. The Huntington Fire Department was formed in 1843, and the Huntington Manor Fire Department sixty years later.

On November 12, 1903, a group of community residents held a meeting resulting in the formation of the Fairground Fire Company, with a membership of thirty-three men. The officers were George Ferguson, Daniel Fleet, William

Murray and Albert S. Pettit. The renamed Huntington Manor Fire Company was incorporated March 1, 1904. Allison E. Lowndes made a gift to the company of a 50-foot lot on New York Avenue on April 2, 1904, for a building site. The estimated cost of the original fire house was $700, and it was necessary to obtain a mortgage from the Bank of Huntington for $600. The building, shown on the photograph below, was completed on August 1, 1904.

The first truck was a hand-drawn cart equipped with buckets, lanterns, rope and one ladder, built at Jackson's Blacksmith Shop at a cost of $125. It was placed in service September 6, 1904. The first piece of motor apparatus was purchased in 1913.

On April 20, 1908, the Huntington Manor Fire Company was divided into two companies, Huntington Manor Hook and Ladder Co. No. 1, and Huntington Manor Hose Company No. 1. It was organized as the Huntington Manor Fire Department, with C. B. Tuttle as the First Chief.

At right: State-of-the-art fire truck in 1916.

A fireman named Marzen was the first member of the Huntington Manor Fire Department to die in the line of duty. The Department was fighting a fire at the Knights of Columbus in the 1930's when he lost his life. His funeral procession on New York Avenue (opposite today's "Big H") is shown below.

The Huntington Manor firehouse that most people remember was built between School and Church Streets in 1922 and enlarged in 1940 (shown below).

SCHOOLS AND TEACHERS

School teachers had an important impact on the residents of Huntington Station, and thus on its history. The school teacher, usually female, was not supposed to be married and was required to live in the town he or she taught in. Teachers were influential in shaping the future of the town's children, but did not always receive proper recognition. They were in a position to make or break a student. Every once in a while a teacher comes along who has a positive influence on students year after year. Their teaching abilities far surpass the average. This is not to deny the importance of a student's ability and effort, but it is widely accepted that some teachers are more effective than others.

1872 RULES FOR TEACHERS

1. Teachers each day will fill lamps, clean chimneys.
2. Each teacher will bring a bucket of water and a scuttle of coal for the day's session.
3. Make your pens carefully. You may whittle nibs to the individual taste of the pupils.
4. Men teachers may take one evening each week for courting purposes, or two evenings a week if they go to church regularly.
5. After ten hours in school, the teachers may spend the remaining time reading the Bible or other good books.
6. Women teachers who marry or engage in unseemly conduct will be dismissed.
7. Every teacher should lay aside from each pay a goodly sum of his earnings for his benefit during his declining years so that he will not become a burden on society.
8. Any teacher who smokes, uses liquor in any form, frequents pool or public halls, or gets shaved in a barber shop will give good reason to suspect his worth, intention, integrity and honesty.
9. The teacher who performs his labor faithfully and without fault for five years will be given an increase of twenty-five cents per week in his pay, providing the Board of Education approves.

One such teacher, Florence E. Welsch, came to Huntington Station in 1932 and became an important asset to generations of residents. She has been not only a teacher but a friend to anyone who needed her. She often found the time and money to help a student in distress. She was a woman ahead of her time, strongly believing in integration before the word was part of our vocabulary.

Florence Welsch expected a lot from her students and usually got their best efforts. I think the reason she was so successful is that she did not treat her profession as a job but as a *responsibility.* Her enthusiasm was contagious, in and out of school. She mingled with the local families and very soon became part of the community. One former student said, "It was as if she had been born here." Even in retirement, she remembers most of her students—not only their first and last names, but also their relatives!

Lillian Bifulco Valentino remembers the first time she saw Miss Welsch. Everyone knew she came from "the city." She was not only beautiful in appearance but also in dress. Lillian still remembers her blonde hair tied in a braided bun. "She was the best teacher I ever had," says Lillian. "She had a warmth and concern for her students and made you feel good about yourself."

In 1940 Miss Welsch married Elmer Bowes, another teacher, and future generations would know her as Mrs. Bowes. Florence and Elmer had a daughter, Pamela. Dr. Pamela Bowes Davis now lives in Cleveland, Ohio. She is Chief of Pediatric Pulmonary Medicine, a specialist in cystic fibrosis, and judged to be one of the best doctors in America.

My favorite story, perhaps apochryphal, about this wonderful woman is how she decided to retire. One day at the beginning of the school year she recognized the last name of one of her new students. She said, "I used to teach your father." "No, you didn't," was the student's reply. "That was my grandfather." Presumably she took that as a sign that it was time to retire. What a shame. The students thereafter would never know the love and respect we had for Florence Bowes. She remains always in the hearts and memories of her students.

When Florence Welsch Bowes first arrived in Huntington in 1932, she had a tour of two schools: Roosevelt Elementary (Agnes Bailey, principal) and Lincoln Elementary (Ernestine Scudder, principal). She said, "Both principals maintained a decorum seldom seen in today's houses of learning. These fine women believed strongly in the work ethic and reminded their charges that 'idle hands make the devil's work.' Both were strict disciplinarians. Moral values, discipline, respect for elders and authority were part of the character-molding process. In one classroom, a dunce cap and stool were still in use. The floors were clean and shining; no papers or graffiti were in the hallways. When the bell rang for passing, children filed out of the rooms quietly and on to recess. Never have I witnessed such control. School started at 8:15, with no "free periods," ½ hour for lunch, and ended at 3:45—a full day of instruction.

Agnes Bailey, Principal of Roosevelt Elementary School

"Every school day opened with the Pledge of Allegiance and the raising of the American Flag. It was a prized honor to be chosen to lift "Old Glory" in the early morning. The adult custodians lowered the flag at sunset. Custodians were not just 'janitors.' They were an integral part of the whole educational process. In addition to keeping the school clean, they were busy supervising delinquent students assigned to cleanup duties, helped to supervise lunch and recess, and were a "big brother" to those who strayed from the school disciplinary process. It seemed that schools were communities in themselves.

"Every assembly began with the Pledge of Allegiance, a reading from the Bible, followed by the Lord's Prayer. Quite a contrast to today's accepted standard." [Note: In 1954, President Eisenhower signed a congressional resolution altering the Pledge of Allegiance. The resolution added the words "under God" between "one nation" and "indivisible." He felt this addition would rededicate the nation to its "divine source." However, in 1962 the Supreme Court held in *Engle v. Vitale,* or the "Regents Prayer Case," that the recitation of a prayer in public schools violated the establishment clause of the First Amendment.]

When we watch our children and grandchildren grow up in schools around the country, and see children carrying weapons in school, it makes you wonder that maybe the *taste* of discipline and a *diet* of respect for elders and authority as a daily routine, *sprinkled* with little prayer now and then, might be just the recipe we need today.

I personally found that the discipline was served with fairness and kindness. When I was in Mrs. Hazzard's 5th grade class, we moved from 1157 New York Avenue to 100 Second Street. This put me out of the Roosevelt School district and into the Lincoln School district. So as not to transfer schools for two years, and change the friends I had made since kindergarten, I kept using my old address. This continued until a new neighbor moved across the street and complained to the principal, Mrs. Bailey, that her daughter had to change to Lincoln School while I was still at Roosevelt.

I was called out of class to speak to Mrs. Bailey. I can still remember standing next to the water fountain in the hall, waiting for her to come around from her office. I can still hear the click of her heels as she came marching down the hall—each click like the beat of my little heart. My knees were shaking. She asked me why I wanted to stay at Roosevelt and why I used my old address. I figured this was it—I'm done for. I remember thinking, *they don't put kids in jail for this, do they*? I don't recall what reasons I gave, but the stern look on her face was gradually replaced by a soft smile. She said, "You're a good student and a good boy, and I'm going to allow you to stay in Roosevelt School." I was speechless. I'm not even sure I said thank you. It may have just been an understanding, or a nod, as she turned around and walked away. For some odd reason, the click of her heels did not seem as ominous as before.

Years after, I would meet her in stores and remind her of this story I knew she would have liked to forget. As an adult, I realized that she wasn't so tough after all. I was, and still am, very proud to have known Agnes Bailey.

When the first schoolhouse was built on School Street in 1906, there were not enough children in the area to fill its four rooms. Since only two rooms were needed, the shutters were closed on half the building *(see photo below)*.

The bell on top of the school has its own story. It originally came from the Union School Building on Main Street in Huntington, across from the Old First Church, and was installed on top of the new school in 1906. According to Jack Abrams, curator of the Huntington District School Heritage Museum, a man was paid $120 a year to ring the bell twice a day. The bell rang half an hour before school started (to tell the children to get to school) and at 3 p.m. (presumably to warn parents that the kids were coming home).

In 1913 the bell and the children were brought to the new Lowndes Avenue School at Lowndes Avenue and School Street. The bell was kept in storage and rediscovered years later by Bill Falcone, a custodian. Dusted off, it was displayed for many years at the Huntington Elementary School. Today the bell is on display in the School Museum located in the Woodhull School, on Woodhull Avenue.

The population of Huntington Station had been growing, and the Lowndes Avenue School had been built in 1913 to accommodate the larger number of children. It is shown in the photograph on the next page. The cost of the new school was $58,000. Although it was much larger than the old School Street school, an addition had to be built in 1926 which doubled the size of the Lowndes Avenue School. The addition, along with renovations to the building, cost $99,409. Upon completion of the construction, the school was renamed Roosevelt Elementary School.

Lowndes Avenue School, 1913

School expanded and renamed Roosevelt Elementary, 1930's. It was torn down to construct the Huntington Elementary School in 1969.

In 1924, the 8th grade class at the Lowndes Avenue School created a publication called *The Milestone.* It is similar to a yearbook, without photographs. Local merchants advertised in it, and a special thank you was given to "all those of the *Long Islander* who freely gave their time and assistance to help make our paper a success." The Editor-in-Chief was Samuel Raskin, the Editor was Dorothy McKee, and the Assistant Editor was Donald Bullyment. Bertha Konglebeck served as Social Editor, Francis Jackson was Business Manager, Joseph Dans was Chief of Reporters, and Editor Dorothy McKee doubled as Secretary.

In an article entitled, "Our Aim," the students explain that the purpose of their paper is "not only to be a Milestone in our school life, but to make our school better known." The article also gives a good account of the growth of Huntington Station schools up to that date, and ends with the students' hopes for a Huntington Station High School in the future.

THE MILESTONE

Lowndes
Avenue
School

HUNTINGTON STATION, LONG ISLAND
Nineteen Hundred and Twenty-Four

Front cover of The Milestone, 1924.

School construction flourished in Huntington Station in the 1920's. The Lincoln Elementary School opened in September 1925 on 9th Street. It is shown in the photo below, taken in 1925.

The Dramatic Club gathers on the front steps of the school, in this photo taken in 1931.

During the World War II years (1941-1945), Huntington Station was involved in doing everything possible for the war effort. This included blood drives, using ration stamps, and buying war bonds. Patriotism was alive and well. School campaigns encouraged students to buy war bonds or stamps, and the U.S. Treasury Department awarded citations to schools that participated in the war-financing programs. Roosevelt Elementary School was no exception, and received many awards for their accomplishments.

A field ambulance was presented to the U.S. Army.

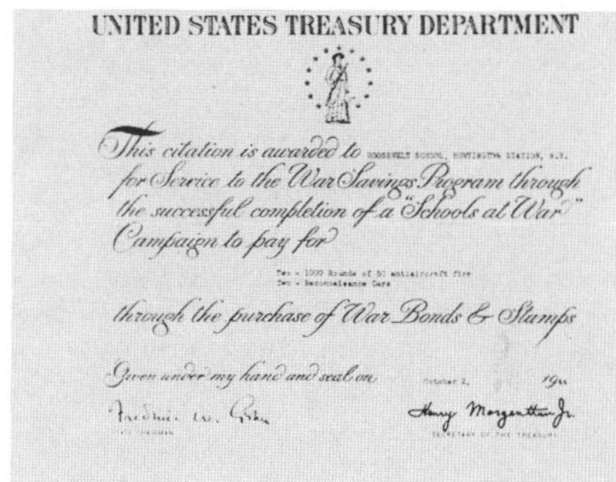

UNITED STATES TREASURY DEPARTMENT

This citation is awarded to ROOSEVELT SCHOOL, HUNTINGTON STATION, N.Y.
for Service to the War Savings Program through the successful completion of a "Schools at War" Campaign to pay for

through the purchase of War Bonds & Stamps

Given under my hand and seal on October 2,

Henry Morgenthau Jr.
SECRETARY OF THE TREASURY

Citation for purchase of two 1000-round cases of 50-caliber ammunition and two reconnaisance cars.

This photograph, taken at Roosevelt Elementary School in 1943, shows sandbags at the right, one of many civil defense precautions taken during World War II.

By 1939, R. K. Toaz Junior High School was under construction at the junction of Nassau Road and Woodhull Road *(see photo below)*. This is the present site of Touro Law School. Before Toaz Junior High was built, Huntington Station children used to call this area "the big woods."

No matter what era your school memories are linked with, some things never change — such as the impossibility of pleasing a child when packing a school lunch:

A MOTHER'S LAMENT

TODAY I ROSE AND PACKED MY SON
A LUNCH A MONARCH WOULD NOT SHUN.
AN ORANGE AND A HARD-BOILED EGG,
A NICE COLD CRUNCHY CHICKEN LEG.
CHEESE SANDWICHES ON SALTY RYE,
A PICKLE, PLUS A PIECE OF PIE.
AND WHAT'S THE REASON THAT I MUTTER?
HE TRADED IT FOR PEANUT BUTTER.

From the Lincoln Elementary School Jotter *(P.T.A. bulletin), circa 1935.*

HUNTINGTON POLICE DEPARTMENT

The original Huntington Police Department was made up of local men. Most were born and raised in the township of Huntington and attended our local schools. Their job was to maintain law and order in a area where they knew most of the people. personally. This fact was both an advantage and disadvantage, but one that they employed to keep peace and tranquility in our small town of Huntington Station.

Violent crime and drugs, now an integral part of our daily lives, were once unheard of in Huntington Station. Violence in those days was generally confined to bar room brawls.

We had police vehicles, though not as many as there are today. The remainder of the force walked beats where they could become acquainted with, talk with, and maintain a close relationship and friendships with the townspeople.

Having this type of police force was like having a professional law and order organization of men with the compassion and understanding of television's Sheriff Andy Taylor of Mayberry—something our present-day law enforcement agencies do not have the luxury of being.

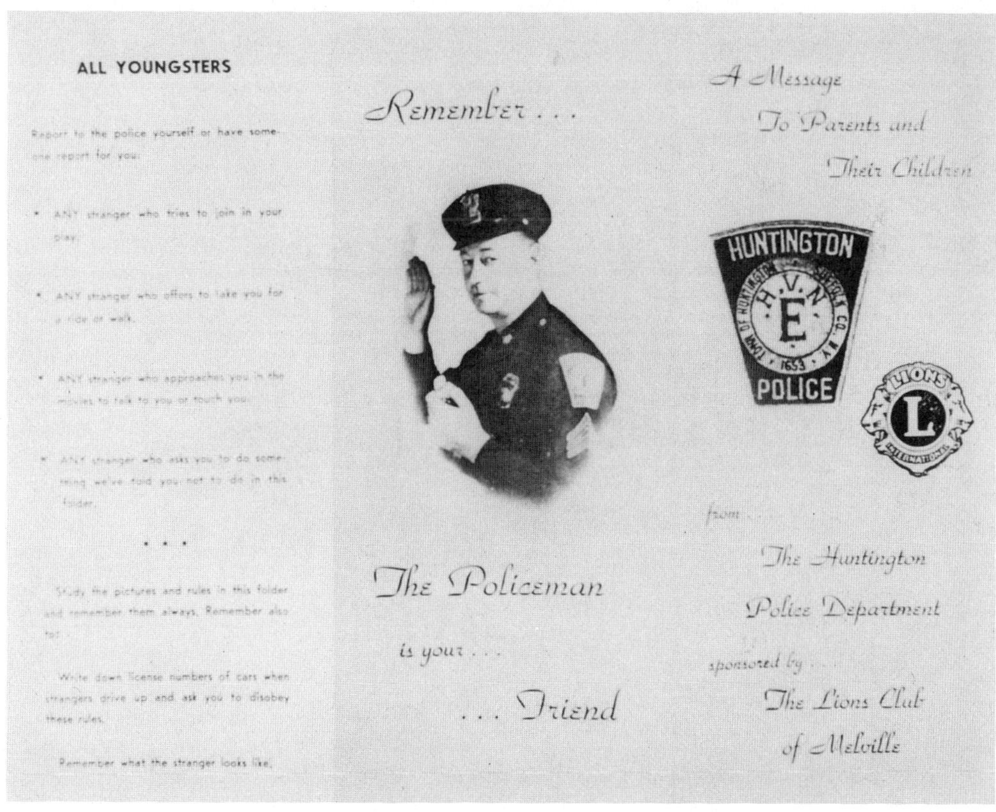

A 1950's brochure distributed to parents and children. The policeman was someone we trusted and respected. Officer on front is William 'Bill' Albin. See next page for other side of brochure.

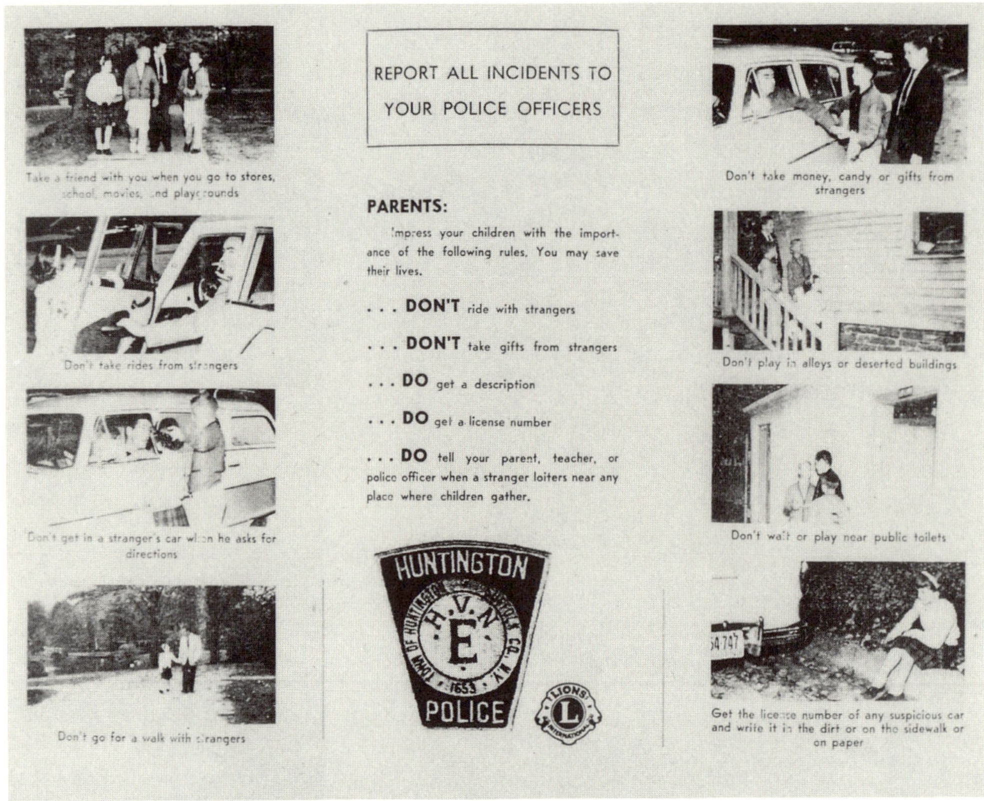
Take a friend with you when you go to stores, school, movies, and playgrounds

Don't take rides from strangers

Don't get in a stranger's car when he asks for directions

Don't go for a walk with strangers

REPORT ALL INCIDENTS TO YOUR POLICE OFFICERS

PARENTS:

Impress your children with the importance of the following rules. You may save their lives.

. . . **DON'T** ride with strangers

. . . **DON'T** take gifts from strangers

. . . **DO** get a description

. . . **DO** get a license number

. . . **DO** tell your parent, teacher, or police officer when a stranger loiters near any place where children gather.

HUNTINGTON
H.V.N.
E
TOWN OF HUNTINGTON SUFFOLK CO. N.Y.
1653
POLICE

LIONS
L
INTERNATIONAL

Don't take money, candy or gifts from strangers

Don't play in alleys or deserted buildings

Don't wait or play near public toilets

Get the license number of any suspicious car and write it in the dirt or on the sidewalk or on paper

When reading the cautions expressed in the 1950's, it's interesting to reflect that every one of the "do's and dont's" still apply today.

Note that the brochure was sponsored by the Lions Club of Melville as a public service.

POLICE DEPARTMENT

HUNTINGTON, NEW YORK

. . . . 19 . .

MR . . . .

YOUR REAR-WINDOW / FRONT-DOOR **WAS FOUND OPEN**

BY OFFICER . . . .

TIME . . . A. M. . . . P. M.

Ray K. Leighton, Chief of Police

The kind of personal attention to people's homes exemplified by this card from the 1950's helps explain why the people of Huntington Station felt a sense of safety in their daily lives.

Edward Johntry of the Suffolk County Police Historical Society gave me a brief history of the Huntington Police. The force began in the 1800's, but for many years consisted of just a handful of men. It was still a very small department until 1954, when the need for policing started to increase. By 1959, the Huntington Police Department had 141 members.

Several people who have contributed their reminiscences of old Huntington Station to the second section of this book have mentioned the "cop's booth," which was a small booth maintained by the Huntington Police at the corner of New York Avenue and Broadway. Their presence added to the sense of security and order in our town.

This was true even in the 1970's, when a Huntington couple I know was traveling west on Route 25A from Locust Valley and a reckless driver almost collided with their car. A few heated words were exchanged between the two drivers, and the couple continued on towards Huntington. Suddenly they realized the other driver was following very close behind, looking furious. They became more and more nervous as they were tailed through Cold Spring Harbor and into Huntington village. At that point the wife said, "I'm afraid to go home — you never know what this man might do. Let's go down to the police booth!" The husband agreed, and they did so. As soon as they parked in front of the booth, the reckless driver took off for parts unknown, and the couple never saw him again.

Unfortunately, the police booth is no more, but the value of a continuous police presence in our communities seems to be making a comeback nevertheless. Recently the Suffolk County Police 2nd Precinct opened an annex on New York Avenue in Huntington Station, a development welcomed heartily by the residents and store owners there.

HUNTINGTON STATION ROTARY CLUB

The organization meeting of the Huntington Station Rotary Club was held October 25, 1945 at Oscar's Willow Pond Inn, Jericho Turnpike. The Station Club was organized with the following charter members (in alphabetical order): John Bertram, Leo Cass, Dodd Craft, William Duesselman, Al Fehleisen, Harry

Fox, Arther Goeller, Edmar Green, George A. Hahn, Theodore Horn, Alfred Jacobsen, John Johnson, Rev. Thomas Judge, Edwin Ketay, George Larsen, Adolph Maggi, Daniel Martin, John Mohlenhoff, Rev. Paul Pallmeyer, Morris Ruthizor, Ben Salee, Paul Schaefer, Nicholas Schwartz, Irving Shear, Lawrence Walsh, and Herman Weinstein.

On December 12, 1945 the Club received its first charter and elected as President Rev. Paul Pallmeyer, pastor of St. Peter's Lutheran Church; as Vice President Dodd Craft, Supervisory Principal of South Huntington School; and as Secretary/Treasurer, Theodore Horn, Superintendent of South Huntington Water District. Other Board Members were Harry Fox, Alfred Jacobsen, Rev. Thomas Judge, and Arthur Goeller.

Back row, left to right: Alfred Jacobsen, Arthur Goeler, Rev. Thomas Judge, Harry Fox. Front row, left to right: Dodd Craft, Rev. Paul Pallmeyer, Theodore Horn.

PART II

REMEMBRANCES OF LIFE IN HUNTINGTON STATION

THE PEOPLE OF HUNTINGTON STATION

What was it like to live in and be a part of the old town of Huntington Station? The people I met while writing this book were informative and sometimes emotional. They all agreed that it was time someone remembered the people of Huntington Station. When I asked Julia Algieri Pipia, "What would you want others to know and remember about our community?" her reply was quick and easy: "The *closeness* of the people." If there was a party, everyone joined in the festivities. If there was a funeral, everyone was there to extend their sympathies.

Once, when Frank Sinatra was singing *The House I Live In (That's America to Me)* in a concert, and came to the part about *"the little town or village where my people lived and died,"* the camera scanned the faces in the audience. Some were serious, some had a slight smile, and all were in deep thought about this wonderful yet imperfect country we live in. No doubt they were remembering their own home towns. Listening to the song, I was having flashbacks of all the people I knew in our town. I'm proud to be an American and to have grown up in a town like Huntington Station. I'm sure you have the same feeling about America, and about Huntington Station or your own hometown.

History is said to be written by the victors. Generals get the credit for winning the war. True, you need competent leaders to win, but it could not be accomplished without the efforts of the common soldiers. In baseball they speak of great managers and the winning pitcher. In football they hail the great quarterbacks. Having these talented people is important, but they need the help and support of the rest of the team. As with all written history, the lives and experiences of the people who lived in the town cannot be separated from the history of the town itself. History is the ordinary people, too, who lived, worked, loved, and died...and never appear in history books.

The personal remembrances in this section may help to recapture the image of the town we once knew and the closeness we had.

FLORENCE BOWES REMEMBERS

I came to Huntington in 1932 as a very young teacher of Social Studies. Robert K. Toaz hired me and planned to place me in Roosevelt Elementary School on Lowndes Avenue in Huntington Station. Agnes Bailey, principal of Roosevelt, informed him she had already hired the previous applicant, so Woodbury Avenue School became my home base for the next seven years. My first principal was J. Taylor Finley.

The Board of Education required all its teachers to live in town. Hence, I roomed and boarded at 91 High Street with a Mrs. Walsh. On weekends I was allowed to go home to see my parents in Bellaire.

Trolley service to the railroad station had been suspended, and the trip from Woodbury Avenue School to the station was a trying one. After my first weekend of trekking up the hill on New York Avenue to the depot, the school custodian, Mr. Flowers, took me up the hill on Soundview Road to the walls of the H. Bellas Hess estate. He introduced me to the gardener, who accorded me the right to cross the estate as a short cut to the railroad station.

Although I lived in a farm area not yet designated a suburb (our backyard was an asparagus farm that stretched for miles), I was struck by the vastness of the Hess Estate and the magnificent plantings of dogwoods, azaleas, rhododendrons, yews, firs, and cedars, as well as many maple and oak trees. Springtime at the Hess Estate was a kaleidoscope of colors, accentuated by the beautiful red, pink and white dogwood trees, and the varied hues of huge azaleas. The house was immense and the walk around it reminded me of baronial estates in Europe. It would have been easy to dawdle and "stop to smell the flowers," had I not had a train to catch. The beauty of this estate is etched in my memory forever.

To the west was Bergen Park, a series of farms run by the Tenutos, Feracos, Menzas and other families. Here was farm life at its best. I taught the children of these wonderful people, and they invited me to their homes on occasion for dinner. Arriving soon after school was dismissed, I was wide-eyed at the size of the farms—the huge truck farm areas, the cows, chickens, pigs, horses—a veritable fiefdom.

I soon discovered that I was to work for my dinner! I arrived at sausage-making time. The pig entrails had been boiled and cleaned, and the meat simmered in a huge pot over an outdoor fire. The older boys were busy at a grinder spewing out steaming meat to be picked up by the girls and me, to be stuffed into the casings draped from a square made from four washpoles. Each ladle, filled with meat, was shoved through the casing with a wooden broom handle. This city slicker had her first taste of farm life.

Florence Welsch Bowes

The dinner was a banquet. I have never been fond of beets. When I was served what in New York City would have been borscht, I gulped twice, remembered my mother's teaching, ("when eating at someone's home, eat what is given you") and said as politely as possible, "This is lovely-looking borscht!" Mrs. Tenuto placed a dollop of sour cream on top and exclaimed, "It's pig's blood soup!" I beat a hasty retreat to the outhouse.

This memorable episode was but the first of many visits to local farms. Weekends saw this city girl bouncing through the Hess estate carrying freshly made Italian bread, eggs, pieces of ham, a milk can full of cream and homemade Italian pastries not to be found in city stores.

Winter in Huntington was an experience never to be forgotten. After the first snowfall, the boys and girls from Bergen Park, Wall Street, and Woodbury Avenue gathered at the top of High and Prospect Streets. The farmers brought bales of hay and stacked them in front of the A&P on Main Street. The Priscos and other families brought their handmade bobsleds, and the evening began. For a while I watched with envy as the Priscos, Sestis, Malicos, Catapanos and Carinos climbed aboard and gave a "heave-ho" down the hill to the hay bales. It was unseemly for a "school marm" to straddle the small bobsled link in a dress suit. But when one father offered me a pair of his dry pants, I was off and sledding.

When the lake at Heckscher Park froze over, the students and I met at the carriage stall on the rim of the lake, put on skates and gleefully played "snap the whip" on the ice. Toasting marshmallows over an open fire polished off the evening nicely.

Old Mr. Hawkshurst, who owned the dairy farm and truck farm, was generous with his hay wagon. He took 85 students on a snowy ride to the University at Farmingdale so we could see the log cabin built by their students. It's a shame that things like that have vanished from the Huntington scene.

In 1933, I was privileged to teach Donald Campbell, later killed in World War II. This young conservationist loved all forms of nature. I was a kindred spirit, and soon the other students and I were tending owls with broken wings, orphaned baby birds, a baby possum left to fend for itself, and a nest of rabbits, hungry and abandoned. On one occasion, Donald brought in a six-foot black snake with a broken vertebrae. We made a cast of wood and plaster of paris, fashioned a cage of chicken wire, and soon it was the mascot of the classroom.

As an exponent of John Dewey, the forward-looking educator of the time, I tried to have the students "learn by doing." Donald had discovered Smith's Pond in Huntington Station, west of Park Avenue and just north of the tracks. After school we would hike to the pond with nets, bottles and boxes to snare tadpoles from the pond and catch butterflies in the surrounding fields of wildflowers.

After my marriage some ten years later, my husband and I went to a Revolutionary War House, long since destroyed, and chiseled out the huge rocks that were part of the foundation. They are today the front steps of our home at 57 Crooked Hill Road. Our street was known as Lewis Avenue, Huntington Station until 1944, when it was renamed Crooked Hill Road, Huntington. When we first moved in, in 1941, electricity had not yet arrived. For several months we dined romantically by candlelight, and preserved our perishables in the basement sinks on 75-pound chunks of ice from the ice dock.

New York Avenue at Huntington Station was a truly rural town. As you walked up from the Gordon & Kerner produce building on the corner of Academy Place, you would pass the upholstery shop, run by a man named Isaac, stop for penny candy at the store just before Sarrow's Market, look at the furniture in Friedman & Haas's window, long for the exquisite bisque dolls in the doll shop (I still own one today), pass some open fields, and come to Levy's Stationary.

Some folks will remember the Tucker car.—a revolutionary postwar automobile shaped like a torpedo, with radical things like seatbelts. This phenomenon made its one and only debut in Huntington Station opposite Sarrows' Market. Scores of people came to gape, but became suspicious of the manufacturer's claims. Shortly after its birth came its demise. It was too advanced for its time.

South of Levy's Stationery was the "clubhouse" or meeting place of the Huntington Station area, Freddie Sforza's shoe repair shop. Chairs outside beckoned the footsore and weary to sit and relax, or to run into Levy's for an ice cream bar and then pass the time watching people go by or engaging in gossip. Freddie was a veritable fountain of knowledge about the local doings.

Further south on New York Avenue and in the midst of this business potpourri stood the *big* store—Ben Franklin Variety Store. It was the Woolworth's of Huntington Station, filled with numerous items to delight the shopper.

A breather or two further south was Carino's Fruit & Vegetable Store, with fresh produce stashed on the sidewalk. As one passed this display of cucumbers, squash, apples and oranges, one's nostrils were assailed by the smell of freshly baked bread and cake coming from Hollis's Bakery next store. Mary Johnson, who tended the wares, was as beautiful as the cakes she sold. Years later, when my mother and father came to live with us, we learned that Mother's favorite haunts were Freddie's Shoe Repair (Fred usually wound up going to Levy's to treat her to ice cream) and the Hollis Bakery, where Mother and Mary would exchange pleasantries.

Just beyond was Diamond's Army & Navy Store. More than once, the Diamonds supplied clothing for the poor children in the area. A step beyond was the downfall for all dieters, Reese's Ice Cream Parlor. Much of the ice cream was made on the premises, and 10 cents bought a triple decker of pure heaven.

Like a child missing front teeth, there came a gap in the businesses until one reached the railroad bridge. This corner of Lowndes Avenue and New York Avenue was the home of Mullen's Hotel (the former North Side Hotel). When it was demolished, a gas station, auto repair and car sales filled the space.

Crossing under the overpass, one came to Concannon's, a coal, kerosene, feed, grain and farm animal store. A more jovial, generous man than Mr. Concannon would be hard to find. When the war years meant supplying your own food or eking out an existence on food coupons, Concannon's sold chickens, turkeys, ducks, hares, suckling pigs etc. with the food to feed them. As a patriotic American, I was one of his constant customers. I raised chickens, ducks, turkeys and guinea hens.

Just further south on New York Avenue was the Huntington Station Library. It was small and compact but widely used by the Station folks as a source of information and pleasure, and was a Godsend to Station children seeking to complete homework assignments.

As with all towns where people lived and died, the Station had its mortuaries. North of the town was the M. A. Connell Funeral Home. South of the town was the A. L. Jacobsen Funeral Home. Both are still at the same sites.

When sitting in Freddie's store, one looked across New York Avenue to the stores on the east side of the road: Walsdorf Insurance, Freedman Jewelers, Harwein Hardware and the proverbial "Deli" where one could find home-made biscuits and the best grade of luncheon meats and cheeses.

The next store was Semon Insurance. John and Anna Semon carried most of the business insurance for the area. In the 1940's John went to the basement of his building to check the furnace. No one knows what went wrong, but there was an explosion and John Semon was burned to death. Anna carried on the business until the chores were too much for her frail body.

Next to Semon's Insurance and on the corner was the "Rock of Gibraltar" of the Station, the Huntington Station Bank. It was a friendly, homey place to conduct one's financial business. Around the corner on Broadway and facing the railroad station was Jacobson's Pharmacy. Harold and Fran Jacobson not only dispensed medications but also cosmetics, perfumes and surgical supplies.

East side of New York Avenue, just north of Broadway. Fire at Semon Insurance (right) killed John Semon.

On the south corner of Broadway there was a little police booth, reminiscent of the Queen's guardhouse at Buckingham Palace. One could always find a friendly officer of the law who saw to it that the peace of the Station was maintained. Ah, nostalgia. In the 30's and 40's, crime was just a word found in city newspapers. Huntington Station's men in blue patrolled the area religiously, giving our citizens a sense of peace and harmony. Men like the Hamilton brothers (Eugene became a deputy inspector), Moon, Scola (an often decorated cop), Juliano, Robinson, Anderson, Richardson and others were visible at the police booth at the railroad station and on the street. Today's police could take a lesson from their dedication to neighborhood solidarity and friendly living.

Thinking of all the stores in Huntington Station reminds me of the diversity of the Station's population. Across from Sarrow's was Levy's Kosher Meat Market, and for a short time a foreign food emporium. Levy's supplied meat for functions at the Jewish synagogue at Woodhull and Spring Street. During World War II the temple offered its offices to the town as a place to donate blood, badly needed by our armed forces overseas. Day after day, the parking lot was filled with cars and trucks; many Huntington and Huntington Station residents were members of the "Gallon Club"—those who gave at least a gallon of blood to save our wounded servicemen. Rabbi Roth was a good neighbor to Toaz Jr. High School. He spent a lot of time there, explaining the place of religion in the lives of people in the town. Flora Raymon ran a used clothing sale at the temple, twice a year, to benefit the community.

Liederkranz Hall, early 1900s, at Woodhull Street and New York Avenue, near Wiggins' Garage.

On the corner opposite the synagogue was a town garage owned by Mr. Wiggins. During the war, the Boy Scouts met in his heated building.

Huntington Station had a lot of social goings-on. Perhaps the busiest place was the VFW Hall, where some kind of activity for large groups was always taking place. Among its workers were Frances and Jerry Downes. The VFW gathered veterans from all areas and kept the spark of service to country and patriotism alive and well. It served as the unifying source for the community for many years.

In the 30's and 40's, before milk came in cartons stacked on supermarket shelves, Pius Schobel made the 4:00 a.m. rounds to deliver bottled milk from his cows pastured on Dunlop Road, to most of the residents of the Station and Village alike. What a sight, on a wintry morning, to see the cream rise out of the bottles, as a result of the extreme cold, and freeze about two inches above the rim of the bottle. No skimmed milk then, only good old-fashioned milk delivered daily. You could also have really fresh eggs delivered for your morning breakfast.

Fire was the enemy in parts of Huntington Station—first John Semon Insurance, and then the apartments above the Ben Franklin Store. Although devastating and leaving several families homeless, it brought into focus the heart and soul of Huntington Station. We may have been a diverse group, but in time of need we were one. In the case of this fire, the shopkeepers offered food, the students from Toaz Jr. High ran a clothing and household utensils drive, and the churches offered aid. Although the losses were substantial, the surviving families were soon relocated with all the trimmings needed to call an abode a home.

In 1934, the 6th, 7th and 8th graders at Woodbury Avenue were putting on Gilbert & Sullivan's *HMS Pinafore*. The cast was ecstatic—the first operetta in the town! But the night before dress rehearsal, I (director, seamstress, producer and the one and only) developed a septic throat. I was too ill to go to school; the dress rehearsal would have to be cancelled. Panic struck the students. One of the girls, fearful her big debut would never take place, showed up at my boarding house with her mother. The mother spoke mostly Italian, and carried two shopping bags overflowing with remedies. I was actually too sick to acknowledge their presence, but the mother kept repeating, "I'm-a gonna fix, no worr!"

Out of the shopping bags came a little sterno stove, a bag of clams, red flannel strips, a blob of goose grease, and a small pot.

In minutes, the small pot with goose grease was cooking on the stove. The clams were opened with a sharp knife, and were wrapped in the red flannel strips. The smell of the grease and the dripping clams wafted down the hallway to the sensitive nose of my landlady. She was quite upset with the odors of my treatment. As she stood by the door to my room, my newly-found Italian friend began to rub my neck with the hot goose grease; then the red flannel and clam mixture was tied around my throat. With a loving hug and an admonition to "leav-a all-a night, come-a out-a good-a inna mornin," this gentle woman packed her bags. With the sign of the cross and a few words, fondling her rosary beads, she vanished with her concerned daughter.

My doctor had ordered bed rest and suggested that I stay out of school for a few days. But what could modern medicine know about my odiferous treatment? Morning found me better, up and washed and off to school. We went ahead with the dress rehearsal, and one night later, the operetta! A Huntington Station woman had saved the day, to the delight of many promising young actors and singers.

Huntington Station folks were "real people." They were friendly, loving, caring, helpful and above all, good neighbors. Who could ask for anything more?

LEON GIMPEL REMEMBERS

I came to Huntington Station in 1946, after World War II. I was employed by the Third Supervisory District at an annual salary of $1800. I was married, and my oldest son, Nolan, was born in November of that year. I moved to School District #3 in 1947. Things started to look up. My salary increased to (wow!) $3000 plus $200 extra for coaching J.V. football and basketball.

However, buying a house was a problem. Banks at the time would only give you a loan on a home if your salary was 25% or more of the purchase price. According to this formula, I couldn't afford a house costing more than $12,000. Decent housing was unavailable at that price in Huntington. I was advised *not* to buy in Huntington Station because it was the "other side of the tracks." The schools were judged "inferior," and I wouldn't meet "the right people." But I had been in the area for two years, and I liked the people I knew there.

Against prevailing opinion, in 1948 I bought the house in Huntington Station that I lived in for the next 25 years. It was on Stratton Drive off 17th Street, a block from Depot Road. Stratton Drive was a dead-end street with three houses on it; one was vacant and the other was occupied by Bill Berhman and his family — excellent neighbors! Later I acquired the property next to me, making a total of three-quarters of an acre on which to indulge in my hobby, gardening. (Today, I still spent 4 to 6 hours daily in my garden.) In those days, I specialized in azaleas and rhododendrons. I had a showcase yard with 50 different named azaleas and 100 named varieties of rhododendrons. Although our house was off the beaten path, many people would drive by in Spring to see the display.

My two sons went to District #13 schools and received an excellent educational foundation. Some of the best teachers I knew worked in that district: Mr. Moore, first grade teacher at Silas Wood Elementary; Mr. Lally, still in the district; Mr. Linquist, high school English teacher, and many more.

There was controversy involving a library to be located on Depot Road around 19th Street..."Should it be built in the Station at all?", "Should it be near a shopping area?" Nevertheless, the library did much to upgrade the area.

Irving Shear, our local pharmacist and a leading citizen, provided medicine for who had lost their jobs and couldn't afford to pay. He carried them, (and me) until they were re-employed. This policy enabled him to open "the big store" at New York Avenue and 11th Street. Later, when Irv opened the Howard Johnson's on Jericho Turnpike and West Hills Road, it was a big event.

I retired to Florida in 1974, but I made many lifelong friends in Huntington Station and never regretted my decision to live "on the other side of the tracks."

SAM LEWIS REMEMBERS

I was born March 9, 1926, in a small coal mining town called Heilwood, in Pennsylvania. Heilwood was originally called *Possum Glory* and later renamed in honor of John Hiel, who started the town. My family moved to Huntington Station in 1927. I guess you could say that makes me almost a native. My father had come to the United States from Abruzzi, Italy, at the age of 16, in the late 1800's. The original spelling of my name was D'Losio. Through a series of missing letters and changed letters, the name Lewis emerged, which was the name on my birth certificate. There were 13 children in my family. I was the youngest.

I enjoyed my early years growing up in Huntington Station. I remember it as a great small town with much to keep kids busy. I loved the town and felt proud to be a part of it. There was always something a country boy like me could do. When I wasn't getting beat up by some older kids, I can remember playing in what we called the "big woods." That's where Toaz Jr. High School was eventually built by the WPA in 1939, on Woodhull and Spring Road (Touro Law School occupies the site now). I used to walk the railroad tracks toward Cold Spring Harbor, which was completely wooded then. It seemed like a long trip. I would shoot crows along the way. I would also walk the tracks in the other direction, toward Greenlawn. At the time there was nothing but farms on both sides of the tracks.

On the west side of New York Avenue at Church Street there was a blacksmith's shop. We spent many an hour watching him shoe farm horses from as far away as Melville. Midway up Church Street was an old synagogue converted to a coat factory called Applebaum's. Later on the coat factory moved to Railroad Avenue. We spent many happy hours playing and making huts out of the huge boxes found around the factory.

Eventually a fire destroyed all the stores in this area except the firehouse. Speaking of the firehouse, one of my first homes—around 1930—was a few doors north of School Street. It was owned by the Raskin family. This house was later demolished and a bandstand built on the site. The Huntington Manor Fire Department Band played every Wednesday night during the spring and summer. My favorite band member was a man I remember only as "Cliff," who sat in the corner playing the harmonica. He had more than a dozen harmonicas of all types. "Cliff" was also the Station street sweeper. He pushed a garbage can on two wheels. With his flip pan and push broom, he would swing the debris over into the can with the greatest of ease. He looked as if he really enjoyed his work. Many times, he would play his harmonica for us as he worked.

"Flash Gordon," another of our local characters, was the fastest-walking person I ever saw. He delivered newspapers and could be seen running up and down New York Avenue. "Flash" was always at the railroad station with a baggage cart to greet the trains. Kids would stop to talk to him, and when asked he would gladly pucker up his lips and do his imitation of a train whistle. Then he'd give out a hearty laugh and continue his run.

Fr. JohnOravecz, 1945.

Father John Oravecz, affectionately called "Father John," was a priest at St. Hugh's Church. Father John made a lasting impression in my life. He was what I called a real person. He was just as much at home on a baseball field, in a bowling alley or a bar as he was in church. In church, he was our priest. Outside the church, he was "one of the boys."

Freddie Specchio owned the Colonial Tavern in Huntington and the Colonial House in Huntington Station, which was just south of the railroad trestle.

The Colonial House, 1956, looking north on New York Avenue.

The Colonial Tavern was a favorite hangout for us World War II veterans (I was in the U. S. Navy Submarines). I remember that Freddie Specchio bought the first Packard in Huntington—his order was in right after the war.

On the north corner of School Street and New York Avenue was an appliance store called Adelman's. In the mid-1930's it had gas pumps in front of the store with overhead hoses that swung over the sidewalk to the curb. The purpose of these hoses was to be able to pump gas without interfering with people walking on the sidewalk. On the south corner of School Street and New York Avenue was Aronson's Gas, which also had overhead hoses.

Overhead gasoline hoses at Adelman's, 1930's; looking north from School Street to New York Avenue.

On the corner of School Street and Lowndes Avenue was Roosevelt Elementary School, named after "Teddy." I remember Miss Scott, Miss Davis, Miss Holdridge and Miss Ludwig. Some went on to teach at Toaz. All the people at Roosevelt Elementary were great, including the janitor, Mr. Miller. Mr. Miller lived on Columbia Street. His son, "Jimmy the Cop," had the number 1 on his badge.

Almost directly across New York Avenue from School Street on the east side of the road was the home and office of Dr. Samuel Teich. Dr. Teich was the son of the people we bought milk from. (There were no Dairy Barns in our day — milk came straight from the cow's udder.) The Teich's dairy was located off Church Street on Academy Place. I remember how proud Sam's family was when he became a doctor.

Former home/office of Dr. Joseph Patiky.

On the same side of the road, north of Dr. Teich's house, was Dr. Joseph Patiky's home and office, on the south corner of Northridge Street. On the north corner was the office of a dentist, Dr. Sam Hollander.

Midway going west on School Street was the VFW Hall. This building was the original School Street school when the town was called Fairground. The only way the VFW could afford to buy the building was to occupy the second floor and rent the first floor to the Huntington Station Post Office. In front of the building was a flag pole and two large cannons, which are still in front of the present VFW building on Pulaski Road. One cannon had the fuse hole plugged, while the other was still active. One of the older kids, Arnold Slessinger, confiscated all our cherry bomb firecrackers and others we called "jackasses" and made the neatest explosive setup we had ever seen. He aimed the cannon at a house across the street occupied by a recluse — a Mr. Schombs, related to the Schombs located on Railroad Avenue. Thank God no one was standing in front of the cannon when it belched out a loud roar and shot the shutters and shingles off the old man's building. What a sight. It was a lot of laughs at the time, but could have resulted in disaster.

The original VFW Hall.

In the early 1930's, we moved from New York Avenue to the corner of Lowndes Avenue and School Street. One of the neighbors was the Kurpita family. The mother raised snakes as pets. We didn't have much money in those days, so we had to invent various ways of scrounging up some coins. Mrs. Kurpita's snakes needed live frogs to eat. We would hike over to Smith's Pond, off Park Avenue, first making sure the older kids weren't around. Then, with pea-sized pebbles and sling shots, we stunned as many frogs as we could, to capture them alive. Mrs. Kurpita would give us a nickel apiece for them.

As with some new enterprises, there was a secondary business that arose out of us trying to capture the frogs. We had to roll up our pants to wade out into the pond to get the frogs. As we returned to shore with our loot, we had leeches all over our legs. We would light up matches or "punks" to remove the leeches, trying to save as many as we could. At the local drug store stood an aquarium filled with live leeches for sale, to be used for various medicinal purposes. What was important to us was that the druggist would give us 5 or 10 cents for every live one we could bring back. It could have been a lucrative business had it not been for the fact that in the process of burning leeches off our legs, a lot of the leeches died.

Further south on New York Avenue was a shoe repairman, Mike Aurricchio. He had three sons, Jimmy, Charlie, and Patsy. Patsy Aurricchio and I were school mates at Roosevelt Elementary School, but lost touch in later years. Pat was killed in World War II; he was only 19 years old.

Columbia Hall was still further south on New York Avenue. It was a dance and catering hall, and they had a lot of weddings there. At one time, the top floor was a basketball court for both men and women. In later years, the first floor was Silberfein's dressmaking shop. The bottom floor was occupied by a stationery store owned by Joe, Margie and John Hulsen. John Hulsen later became the Town Leader. Afterwards the store became a local variety store called Popkin's.

After World War II an amazing car came onto the market — the Tucker. In addition to regular headlights, it had a "cyclops eye" headlight in the middle that moved in the same direction you turned the steering wheel. The son of the owner of Sarrow's Grocery was supposed to have the Tucker agency, but Habberstad got the dealership. Only one was ever delivered to Huntington Station, and it was displayed at Hunt and Mooney's garage.

Hunt and Mooney's in 1935, with Mascaro's Bar and Grill (Venice Hotel) next door. Below: Same buildings today.

Preston T. Tucker was a man ahead of his time. He had dreamed of designing and manufacturing the finest automobile ever made. In the 1930's Tucker saw the war clouds gathering, and he designed a combat car. It was capable of going 100 mph—"too fast" for the Government, which had set a speed limit of 35 mph. But Tucker's combat car had a power operated gun turret on top, and its use on our fighter planes probably saved the lives of many American boys. Tucker's postwar "Torpedo Car" was a revolutionary design. Besides the third headlight, the car was aerodynamically designed, had disc brakes, fuel injectors, torque converters on every wheel, a padded dash, shatterproof glass, pop-out windows, and seat belts. His statements that the Big 3 car dealers had no regard for safety made many enemies. For example, they wanted seat belts eliminated because it implied that cars were unsafe. There was an implication that they took Tucker to court (he was found not guilty) because he had made the car "too good." It would have cost other car makers millions just to catch up. They stopped at nothing to keep him from building his car. Although only 50 of them were ever produced, 46 are still roadworthy and in use today. And many of Tucker's innovations are found in the cars we drive in the 1990's.

On the corner of Fairground Avenue, Depot Road and Pulaski Road was the 5-Corner Diner. This diner holds a special place in my heart. There I was introduced to a girl named Viola ("Vi") Griffin, whom I eventually married. We had seven children: Sam Jr., Lorelei, Valerie, Nicky, Stephen, Neil and Kevin. I lived in Huntington Station until September, 1994. I hated to leave town, but after two heart attacks I needed a slower paced life and less real estate taxes—not necessarily in that order. I left behind good friends, my brothers and sisters, my VFW comrades, and also my old fishing buddies, especially Jack DiGiorgio. But I'll always have my wonderful memories of this town.

Diner, interior view.

ANDY COSCIA REMEMBERS

I moved to Huntington Station from what they called "Hells Kitchen" which was located on the upper west side of Manhattan's 10th Avenue. When anyone asked where I was moving, I would say "to the country." That was no lie, *it was the country*! The paper boy threw the newspaper on the lawn, the milkman made deliveries and you could actually see the cream on top of the milk. Doctors made house calls in those days, carrying their little black bags. It was a place to raise children in a safe and healthy environment. The air was fresh and clean from the abundance of trees and growth on land untouched, perhaps, since God's creation.

We were completely surrounded by farms that grew every vegetable one could think of, and were famous for Long Island potatoes. I remember the migrant workers harvesting the potatoes from the fields by hand. When the workers finished picking the surface potatoes, the owners would allow the local residents' children to pick whatever was missed by the workers for themselves. I recall my children doing this; it was fun for them and we enjoyed watching them on their hands and knees digging for those hidden potatoes.

Huntington Station was a quiet town. Trolley cars once operated from Huntington Station to Halesite. (Years after this service was discontinued, you could still see the tracks even after they were covered with black top.) I remember hearing the clickety-clack of the train wheels on the tracks, along with the long sad whine of the whistle from the engine. This alone was a part of being "country." Traffic on weekdays was less than the traffic on Sunday today.

The United States saw hard times during the Depression and war years, and Huntington Station was no exception. Our town was outstanding in that we had the American Legion, the VFW, the Boy Scouts, and many other organizations that performed successful drives for the war effort. We were then, and I believe we still are, a very proud and patriotic community that can rise to any occasion.

Huntington Station had special people, like Mickey Norton (whose father was director of the YMCA) and Charlie Boccia. They devoted their time and effort to make our town noted for its athletics and competitive sportsmanship. They gave people a chance to indulge in all sports by organizing leagues in baseball, softball, basketball, tennis, and whatnot. No one knows this better than our own Bobby Wine, who went to the big leagues and now is a coach with the New York Mets baseball team.

The stores that once illuminated the Station were a pleasure in themselves. Just to mention a few: Freddie's Shoe Repair, Harwein's, Farrell's, DeRosa's Fish Store, and Reese's Ice Cream Parlor.

Another landmark was Gerlick's Hotel, later the Colonial Inn. The steps to the hotel are still there, just south of the railroad trestle. Here the "city folks" who visited friends in "the country " could stay overnight for a dollar or two. Meals could be had at the Trolley Car Diner (Boyle's Diner) diagonally opposite the hotel. A second cup of java was usually on the house.

Gerlick's Hotel in 1935.

These were the days when we only knew of drugs through prescriptions. The taking of drugs for pleasure was unheard of, and the muggers and drug dealers weren't born yet. When I see the problems we are having today in communities across America, all I can say is *God bless what we had in Huntington Station.*

HERBERT HAAS REMEMBERS

My father, Robert Haas, was born in 1900 in Vienna, Austria. He came to the United States, met and married Helen Kleinman (born in the Bronx in 1904). In 1925 they moved to Huntington Station and had three children, Millicent, Sandra and me. We lived on Tower Street right behind Roosevelt Elementary School.

In 1925, my father and his brother-in-law Alvin Friedman, with money borrowed from my mother's parents, bought a furniture and hardware business. The former owner, Charles Brenner, had established the business at the turn of the century. Charles Brenner had two sons, Charles, who opened another furniture store in East Northport, and Harry, who later became District Attorney of Suffolk County.

Alvin Friedman and my father expanded the original furniture and hardware business to include appliances. Three businesses in Huntington Station, located near each other, all sold appliances but each had different name brands, (Aronson's, G.E. & Norge; Adelman's, Kelvinator; and Friedman & Haas, Crosley). Alvin and his wife Rose lived above the store. This successful business survived urban renewal and moved to 1850 New York Avenue. My father continued in the business until his death in 1985. I still have the original safe and cash register they used.

Friedman & Haas, 1935, next to Huntington Manor Fire Department.

Friedman & Haas, 1960's. Robert Haas standing in doorway.

Huntington Station was a special town to grow up in. I attended Roosevelt Elementary, Toaz Junior High, and Huntington High School. At Roosevelt, I remember Miss Scott, Miss Pemperton (Mendelson), Miss Smith, Miss Ormand, Mrs. Granitz (Fairmount), and Miss Stoneman. Mrs. Bailey, the school's principal, was feared by everyone. Rumors abounded that she had a horse whip in her room and that few who got into trouble came out alive. Obviously untrue, but it kept everyone in order. This so-called "rumor" continued for many generations until her retirement.

The playground was our meeting place. You weren't allowed to just "hang out." If you weren't playing with your next door neighbor, (mine was Harold Beres), you gathered with friends on the playground in back of Roosevelt Elementary. You could always find 18 guys to play a game of baseball. The most western section was our basketball court (dirt, of course). The basketball net was made of chain, and the backboard was metal with holes looking like a pegboard. We played soccer using the cross pipes as our goal posts. In May we had Field Day, with games and races. The school was divided into two teams, red and blue. On Arbor Day one year, I remember reciting "Trees" by Joyce Kilmer, on the side of the school.

We also had concerts at Roosevelt Elementary School. My friend Robert Gottlieb played the piano. After his performance, I played the accordion. In those days I was so skinny that the accordion — with only two shoulder straps — kept sliding off my shoulders. Bob helped me by adding a third strap to hold the two shoulder straps together so I could play.

For a penny a day we received a small bottle of milk and a graham cracker at 10 o'clock in the morning. As a reward if we were "real good," we had the privilege of clapping the chalk out of the blackboard erasers in the courtyard behind the building. To this day I'm not sure whether this should have been considered a reward or a punishment.

In those days it snowed a lot every winter. The snow was always piled high in front of my father's store in town. During Christmas time the teachers would take us out caroling to homes along Tower Street, Lowndes Avenue, Columbia Street and Railroad Avenue.

Winter time also meant winter sports. Sledding was best on Tower Street, for both youngsters and their parents. Residents would come from all over Huntington Station just to zip down the hill. The advantage of Tower Street was that we could sled in two directions; one side of the hill descended towards Lowndes Avenue, and the other sloped towards Columbia Street. On the corner of Columbia Street and Tower Street was Miklik's Dairy and what we called Miklik's Hill. Occasionally we would sled down this hill, in and out of the trees. This required more skill, and a lot of sledders were injured when they collided with trees. Rose Miklik Shoebel later ran the dairy farm and moved it to Dunlop and Lake Road, in Greenlawn.

On McKay Road was a chicken farm with a pond in front called Blackshaws Pond. Here we would ice skate and play hockey, and light fires to keep warm. (Of course, we weren't supposed to play with matches. Remember your mother telling you that?)

Then the spring thaw would come, and because the school playground was all dirt, the mud got so thick you could lose your shoes walking through it.

The dirt playground in back of Roosevelt Elementary School. The boys' entrance was on the left, and the girls' entrance was on the right.

How well I remember the Huntington Station Movie. Mr. Mele was the manager. For five cents, your parents dropped you off at 12 o'clock and picked you up at 5 o'clock — our version of the modern day-care center. For a nickel we saw a double feature, a travelogue, cartoons and the Three Stooges. Also on the screen was a bicycle race. The racers had numbers on their backs corresponding to numbers held by children in the audience. If your racer won, you won a prize. You could always which kids had been at the movies on Saturday afternoons. They were the ones squinting at the sun because they had been in the dark for five hours.

When I got to Toaz Junior High, Henry Flynn was our gym teacher. During the World Series, he would broadcast the game on loud speakers in the gym. We were allowed to leave class to hear the game. Mr. Flynn didn't have to worry that some students might leave the building instead of going to the gym; their parents would have been notified right away, and they would have been in big trouble.

After graduating from college, I attended Brooklyn Law School. During the summers I worked for a local law firm, Raskin, Mascaro, Weber & Pallmeyer. Sam Raskin had started his law practice about 1937, and soon teamed up with Harry Lesne. When their partnership ended, Sam and three other town lawyers formed a new firm, Raskin, Mascaro, Weber & Pallmeyer. The firm eventually had three associates, Sol Gordon, Fritz O'Mara and me. By the mid-1960's, the firm had only two partners and was called Raskin & Haas.

When urban renewal demolished the town of Huntington Station, Raskin & Haas moved to its present location on 34 Dewey Street. Sam Raskin retired in 1971. With great respect for his memory, to this day the sign in front of the building still includes Sam Raskin's name.

DR. ROBERT M. GOTTLIEB REMEMBERS

My grandparents, Joseph and Rebecca Aronson, came to America from Russia in 1906. They had six children, Sadie, Ann (my mother), Ida, Betty, Bernie and Jack. When my mother grew up, she married Emanuel Gottlieb. I was born in New York City, but have lived in Huntington and Huntington Station all my life. Our first family home was at 67 Northridge Drive in Huntington Station.

Originally, my grandfather ran a hardware business. The business later expanded to furniture and appliances, and then became a furniture establishment called Aronson's Furniture, at 1071 New York Avenue. My grandfather lived over the store before his children married. In the back of the property was a barn where he kept his horse and buggy.

In later years my uncles, Bernie and Jack Aronson, and my father, Manny Gottlieb, joined my grandfather in the business.

One of my early memories is of going with my grandfather on his collection rounds, where he would collect a dollar or two from everyone who bought furniture on time. Every account was either on paper or in his head — no computers to keep his accounts organized.

There were no school buses then, and I remember walking to school from Northridge Drive. We had two streets to cross. One was New York Avenue opposite Dr. Teich's home office, and the second was Lowndes Avenue and School Street. The name of the school crossing guard at Lowndes Avenue was Mr. Byrnes.

Our school, Roosevelt Elementary, was a two-story building with a basement, built in 1913. Additions were made in 1927. The basement had the boys' and girls' lavatories, the heating plant, and also served as our gym on rainy days. We used to play dodge ball and "steal the ham, steal the bacon." The latter was a game where we chose up two sides with a chalkboard eraser in the middle. Two students met in the middle around the eraser. The idea was to steal the eraser and make it back to the group without being caught by the opposite side.

The first floor contained the auditorium. and also had rooms for kindergarten through third grade and a "special class." The kindergarten was the room in the front of the building. I remember the open cupboards where we used to store our "rugs" for our morning naps. The teacher, Miss Scott, would sometimes play the piano while the class tried to jingle a beat with triangles, bells, drums, and a tambourine.

The auditorium was a multipurpose room. We assembled to salute the flag and say the Lord's Prayer, a tradition questioned in recent years. There was a balcony that could be reached from the second floor. The auditorium served as our meeting place for concerts and plays, and also as a place to eat lunch. It had wooden connected chairs with a flip-up seat. When everyone got out of their chairs at once, the noise of all those seats snapping up made it sound like the building was going to fall down.

The second floor was for grades 4 through 6 and also had the office of the principal, Mrs. Bailey. You froze in your tracks when you heard her footsteps coming down the hall. Because I was a constant talker in class (especially with Ronald "Timmy" Smith), I was a frequent guest in her office. There was something hanging on the wall. It was probably an ornamental piece, but we had all heard from secondhand sources that it was a whip. None of us were willing to do anything to find out firsthand whether she actually whipped anyone.

I was captain of our safety patrol. We gave out summonses for various offenses. If you had too many summonses you were sent to Mrs. Bailey's office — a place we tried to avoid at all costs. Frankie Fry held the record for most summonses.

After school, we walked home, changed our clothes and walked back to the school to play baseball or football. The school playground had two levels. The larger upper area was for the older children, and a smaller, lower level was for the younger children. The playground was all dirt. In the 6th grade, I ran for president on a platform to have grass planted on the playground for a football field. Although I was elected president, I was never able to get the grass planted.

The two-level playground at Roosevelt Elementary School, 1950's.

On the northwest corner of Lowndes Avenue and School Street was Jones' candy store. Actually, it was more like a wooden shack with a covered drive through. In front there were two gas pumps. Inside, there were stacks of all kinds of candy to satisfy a youngster's craving for sweets. One that I remember in particular was long sheets of paper pasted with colored sugar dots that you bit off, sometimes biting the paper too.

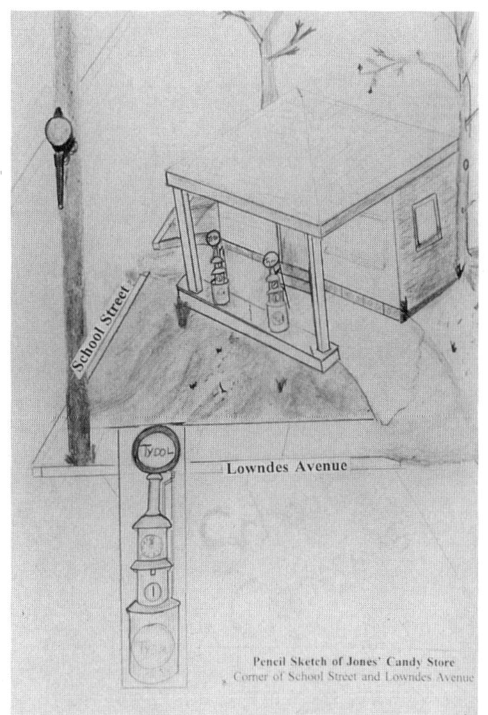

At right: Pencil sketch of Jones' Candy Store, Lowndes Avenue and School Street.

SNAPSHOTS OF HUNTINGTON STATION LIFE

From Bill Amadio:

In the early part of the century, Fusaro's Brickyard had huts on Fusaro Beach for the laborers to live in. My mother was born there, and her family moved to Railroad Avenue about 1915. She told me that St. Hugh's Church was only used during the summer; after Labor Day she had to go to St. Patrick's.

Huntington Station was one big dairy farm in those days. There was the Teich Dairy at Hillside Avenue (now Academy Place) adjacent to Church Street. Mr. Teich sold the farm to Pete Schobel about 1935, and he renamed it Hillside Dairy. Pete married Rose Miklik, and moved the Miklik Dairy Farm to Columbia Avenue. Then there was Albert's Dairy on Broadway, and Sherman Fleet's Dairy — his pasture was on Olive Street.

Cantrell's Auto on Pulaski Road made wooden bodies for early General Motors station wagons. I *recall many railroad flatcars carrying chassis to Cantrell's to have the bodies put on.*

Portable radios were not available, and most people couldn't afford a car radio. As they passed Freddie's Shoe Repair they called out questions about the baseball game. The Brooklyn Dodgers' ball scores were available immediately; you could get Yankee scores from Freddie too, but not the Giants — unless the Dodgers had beaten them.

From Vincent and Phyllis Gigante:

As trains pulled into the depot, the trainman would often throw shovelfuls of coal on the ground to be picked up by children and used to heat their homes.

There was a sign in DeRosa's Fish Store stating, "Checks cashed only if accompanied by parents 95 or older."

From Barbara Sforza:

In my early years, our phones had no dials or buttons. You picked up the receiver and a woman would say, "Number, please." She always sounded like she was holding her nose. Phone numbers usually had four digits, like "5836" or "0007." A party line had two or more users on the same number, each identified by a letter, like "2363-J." Being cheaper, this service enabled a lot of people to have a phone. It also gave gossips another source of information, since you could pick up the phone and eavesdrop on a complete conversation.

From an anonymous resident:

Movie newsreels were an important source of information for us. In between films they would show "The Eyes and Ears of the World," about World War II, politics and sports. We also had "singalongs," where a recorded group was singing and you could join in by following the "bouncing ball" on the screen which showed the words of the song.

DR. ALFRED V. SFORZA REMEMBERS

My father, Alfred A. Sforza — better known as "Freddie the Shoemaker," was born in Brooklyn on July 13, 1914. While he was growing up, he often visited his sister in Huntington during the summer. In 1934 his brother-in law-died, and Dad took over his shoe repair business in Huntington Station. My mother, whose maiden name was Lena Bifulco, was born and raised in Huntington. Her father died in 1918, leaving his widow with six small children to raise alone. My mother and father met in 1934, and they were married November 29, 1936.

Fred and Lena Sforza, 1940s.

I was born in Huntington Hospital on August 26, 1939. The bill was $45.00 — about two weeks of my father's wages. I went to Roosevelt Elementary, Toaz Junior High and Huntington High School (a.k.a. R. L. Simpson High). I left town only to attend college, and had no doubt that I would return to Huntington to practice my chosen profession, dentistry.

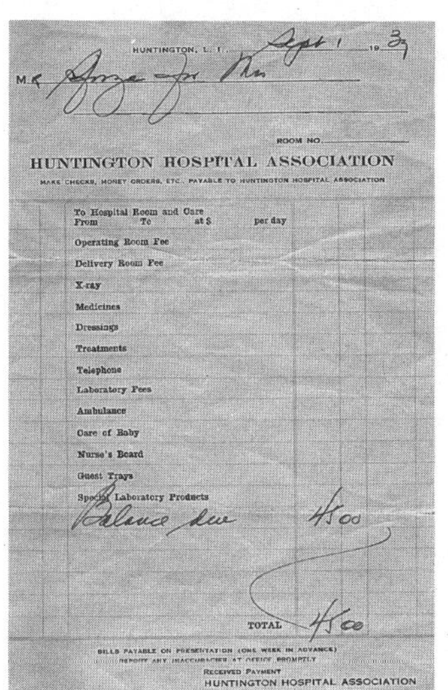

HUNTINGTON, L. I. Sept 1 1939

ROOM NO.

HUNTINGTON HOSPITAL ASSOCIATION

MAKE CHECKS, MONEY ORDERS, ETC., PAYABLE TO HUNTINGTON HOSPITAL ASSOCIATION

To Hospital Room and Care From To at $ per day
Operating Room Fee
Delivery Room Fee
X-ray
Medicines
Dressings
Treatments
Telephone
Laboratory Fees
Ambulance
Care of Baby
Nurse's Board
Guest Trays
Special Laboratory Products
Balance due 45.00

TOTAL 45.00

BILLS PAYABLE ON PRESENTATION (ONE WEEK IN ADVANCE)
REPORT ANY INACCURACIES AT OFFICE PROMPTLY

RECEIVED PAYMENT
HUNTINGTON HOSPITAL ASSOCIATION

Hospital bill from 1939; compare this with the cost of a delivery today!

Huntington Station will always be *my kind of town*. It is sad to think that most people don't know where the town existed. Some don't even know *that* a town existed. Today, when I stop at the traffic light at Broadway and New York Avenue, I often think of how our lives centered around this area. It supplied most of what we needed. We used to say we were going "up to the Station" or "down to the Village," because Huntington Station is on high ground, and to get to the Village you walk downhill.

We walked everywhere. My father walked to work. We walked to town and to school. Although we had a car, it was only used on Sundays to visit relatives. Everyone I knew had either a Schwinn or Columbia bicycle with fat whitewall tires. My bike had a square basket hanging on the front handlebar to hold that loaf of bread or head of lettuce my mother sent me to town to buy. The basket would not stay square for very long. A few falls from the bike easily made a beautiful square basket into a bent and twisted mess. As I got older, it wasn't "kool" to have a basket on your bike (only girls did). I took off the basket and carried the loaf of bread under my arm like a football. Now that was "kool." The bread may have been flattened by the time I got it home, but what mattered was to be a "kool kat."

The 40's and 50's were great times to be alive and living in Huntington Station. Those years were my "good old days." There was a feeling of optimism. People just felt good about themselves. They cared about each other and respected each other's feelings. The mood of living in a small town, and in America, is reflected by the songs we sang and listened to.

In the 1940's, we were just coming out of the Great Depression and were becoming involved in another world war. The Japanese bombed Pearl Harbor on December 7, 1941, "a date which will live in infamy," and our boys, each known as *G. I. Joe*, were going *Over There.* Fathers, sons and brothers were leaving for Europe and the Pacific. And while over there, they were concerned about their women at home, and told them *Don't Sit Under The Apple Tree* with anyone else 'till they came marching home.

Patriotism was at its height. Groups in Huntington Station donated everything they could for the boys overseas. We had War Ration Books with stamps:

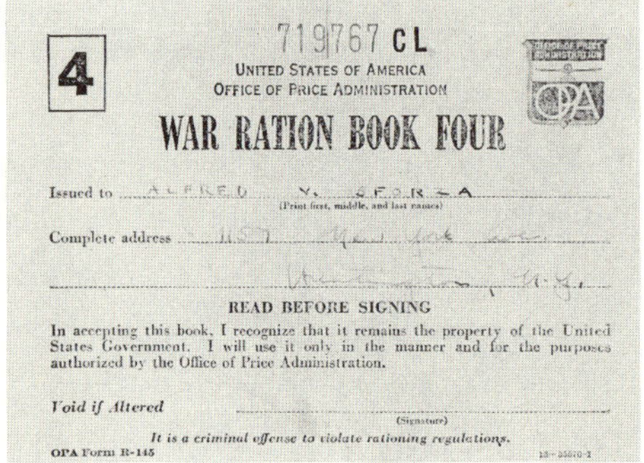

4

719767 CL

UNITED STATES OF AMERICA
OFFICE OF PRICE ADMINISTRATION

OPA

WAR RATION BOOK FOUR

Issued to ALFRED V. SFORZA
(Print first, middle, and last names)

Complete address

READ BEFORE SIGNING

In accepting this book, I recognize that it remains the property of the United States Government. I will use it only in the manner and for the purposes authorized by the Office of Price Administration.

Void if Altered ______________ (Signature)

It is a criminal offense to violate rationing regulations.

OPA Form R-145

Front of ration stamp book, 1943.

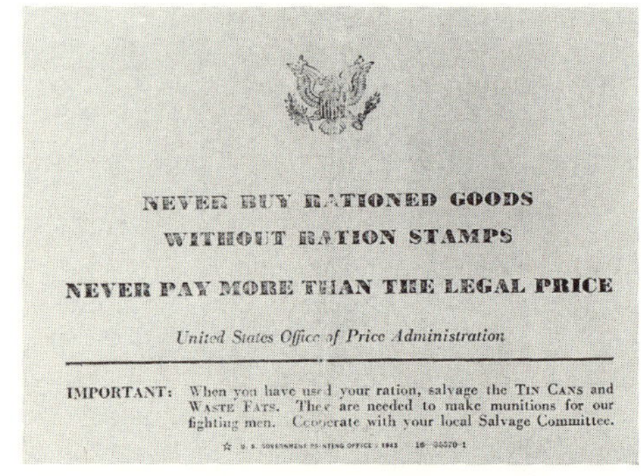

NEVER BUY RATIONED GOODS
WITHOUT RATION STAMPS

NEVER PAY MORE THAN THE LEGAL PRICE

United States Office of Price Administration

IMPORTANT: When you have used your ration, salvage the TIN CANS and WASTE FATS. They are needed to make munitions for our fighting men. Cooperate with your local Salvage Committee.

Back cover, with warning about black marketeers.

We saved tin cans, string, and even the tin foil from gum wrappers. They said *You Made Me Love You* and *I've Got My Love To Keep Me Warm*, and love and marriage was '*Til the End of Time* and for *Always.* It was wiser than *Makin' Whoopie.* They did things like the *One O'Clock Jump* and *Stomping At The Savoy*, and cutting a rug at the *Woodchoppers' Ball.* They jitterbugged to the instantly recognizable sound of Patty, Maxene and LaVerne, dressed in "zoot suits" at dance contests in the Huntington Station Theater with the *Boogie Woogie Bugle Boy* of Company B. Familiar names were Bing, Frank, Glen, Benny, Harry, and Satchmo. They dialed phone numbers like *Pennsylvania 6-5000,* drank *Rum and Coca-Cola* and greeted each other with *Give Me Some Skin My Friend.* "Rosie the Riveter" was part of the female sexual revolution. Everyone wanted more than just a *Kiss To Build A Dream On,* but never stopped doing things to help the community.

When our boys returned home from the war, the nation was still wondering (ever since World War I) *How're You Gonna Keep Them Down On The Farm, After They've Seen Par-ee?"* Although they said *Don't Fence Me In,* their outlook for the future was *I Can Dream Can't I?*

The 1950's were good times in America, and business was booming in Huntington Station. The town provided a healthy environment, and gave us a solid foundation for the rest of our lives. People were considerate and respectful. Eisenhower was president, and as he promised, put a halt to the Korean War. It was a time of great patriotism, second only to the 1940's. It was America, first, last, and always, right or wrong. Crew cuts were "kool." Then the Rock 'n Roll era began. Familiar names were Elvis, Bill Haley, The Platters, Buddy Holly and the Crickets, "Big Bopper" (J. P. Richardson), Richie Valens, Dion and the Belmonts, The Four Lads, and Little Richard. A man named Fats Domino led to a Chubby Checker. The Stroll led to more athletic dances like the Twist. Movies reflected the theme that parents never understood teenagers.

Our songs helped to make those days the best days of our lives. There was an *Affair To Remember* in a *Heartbreak Hotel* with a *Stranger In Paradise.* We called our best girl *My Special Angel,* who was only *Sweet Little Sixteen,* and brought her to the Senior Prom dressed in *A White Sport Coat And A Pink Carnation.* We would *Rock Around The Clock, At the Hop,* in our *Blue Suede Shoes,* to that *Rock and Roll Music,* until the *Wee Small Hours Of The Morning.* Our *Shake, Rattle and Roll* dances were held in the high school gym. There was certainly a *Whole Lotta Shakin' Going On.* The theme of our teen years was *Let The Good Times Roll.* Everything was *Cherry Pink and Apple Blossom White.* We did strange things like "make out." Make out what? We were just *A Teenager in Love,* affected by *Love Potion No. 9.* We would tell our *Young Love,* you are my *Earth Angel,* and *I'm In The Mood For Love,* and that *I'll Never Stop Loving You.* She would say, *Johnny B. Goode.* You can *Love Me Tender,* on *Blueberry Hill, In The Chapel In The Moonlight,* but *Don't Be Cruel.* We would say *I Believe* that *Memories Are Made Of This.* If you were wondering what your *Chances Are* without promising a *Band Of Gold* and a trip to the *Chapel of Love* — probably *The Twelfth Of Never.* Oh well, *Ain't That A Shame. Que Sera, Sera, Whatever will be, will be.* In the 1960's, love and marriage went from *'Til The End Of Time* to *Please Release Me.* Love was supposed to be better the *Second Time Around.* Our burden in life felt like *Sixteen Tons*, but later in life we learned that *Little Things Mean A Lot.*

The 1950's created a new term: *juvenile delinquent.* Rock 'n Roll was accused of creating juvenile delinquents. If we continued to listen to this music and watch that singer wiggle his hips and legs we would be nothin' but a *Hound Dog* and end up on a *Jailhouse Rock. That'll be the Day. Rock 'n Roll* was *Here to Stay*

Just how good the 1950's were is reflected by the success of the cable network Nickelodeon (Nick at Nite) which promotes "Classic TV" and broadcasts shows like "I Love Lucy" and "Dragnet." It reflects a desire to return to a simpler, safer, more orderly time, especially with the high-speed life of today. Perhaps the 1950's were not a better time and fathers didn't always know best, and maybe Desi didn't love Lucy forever, but it did give us something to *strive* for. The values they portrayed were everything that people wanted a family to be.

The 1960's brought a rebellion against rules and regulations. We protested everything imaginable — sometimes just for the sake of protesting. We developed this *need for confrontation*, on things as simple as the temperature on the thermostat. We were ready to confront any person, about anything, at any time. We became angry about many things. We started the 60's with "Ask not what your country can do for you, ask what you can do for your country," and went downhill after that. I have a feeling that before the 1990's end, we will regain faith in ourselves and in our families. We must learn to live in peace and harmony in our community and in our world.

After living in several apartments, my parents were finally able to buy a home at 100 Second Street. Second Street was the first street south of the railroad tracks, on the east side of New York Avenue. Our neighborhood was well integrated. On our small street alone there were Italian, Jewish, Norwegian, German and Black families. The neighborhood was friendly, and we all got along. Our street was lined with oaks and maples, and the lawns were kept neat and trimmed. In the fall, there was always the wonderful smell of burning leaves.

I remember warm summer days, the occasional whisper of the wind through the trees, the sweet smell of honeysuckle, crickets clicking their songs in the woods, the "heat bugs" humming early in the morning, warning us of another hot day, and walking barefoot though the cool green grass in our backyard. Today, a deep breath and just the memory of honeysuckle has almost the same calming effect on me as it did then. Spring and summer, we played baseball. The older kids played at Manor Field, on the east end of Second Street. It had three baseball diamonds: one hardball and two softball fields. One softball diamond had lights for night games. We made some of our sports supplies. Our ball was a former baseball; the remnants of its original cover were wrapped with black electrical tape. Our basketball net was the top half of a wooden produce basket (from

Gordon-Kerner Wholesale Fruit and Vegetable at the corner of Academy Street and New York Avenue), nailed to the side of our garage.

When we were younger, we played baseball in an open lot on the corner of Third Street and Fairground Avenue, alongside St. Peter's Church. Everyone, someday, wants to return to the place of their childhood. One day I decided to drive through my old neighborhood to reminisce. Everything seemed the same, yet different and strange. Our "baseball field" was now overgrown with weeds and looked much smaller. Some houses were the same, but others were broken down, with ill-kept lawns, still others had burned and were never restored. Where did the pride go? So very sad. And something was missing. My four-year-old grandson, who was in the car with me, looked at my old home and said, "Does anyone still live here?" *That's* what was missing — the street and homes didn't look lived in anymore. Where were the green trees that lined the road? Where were the hedges that surrounded the front yard? The azaleas, the forsythias, the rhododendrons? Where were the flowers my mother planted and the rose bush in the front yard that attacked my father when he tried to move it? All gone. In a shoddy attempt to make their properties cheap to maintain, absentee landlords had removed most of the landscaping.

Our five senses: *Sight, Sound, Smell, Taste, Touch.* Extraordinary abilities, and taken for granted unless we lose them. Our senses have many purposes. An obvious one is to supply us with skills. Another is the instant gratification we receive from the sound of a bird singing, the scent of a pine tree, or the sight of a Colorado blue sky over a snow-covered mountain range. Still another is to provide us with an instant flashback to experiences and memories. Early one morning while on a vacation, I was awakened by the long sad sound and echo of a train whistle and the clicking of the wheels against the tracks. Magically I was transported many years into the past to my home on Second Street. I remembered steam engines puffing through the depot, the clanging of the bell, and waking up to the sound of trains and my clock radio with "Jack Sterling in the Morning." I remembered walking by the tracks — those creosote-soaked railroad ties with small stones in between. These visions gave me a wonderful sense of belonging.

We played Cowboys and Indians. In those days, it was hard finding someone to play the Indians. (Today, with the Foxwood Casino in Connecticut, everybody wants to be an Indian.) Our club, The Junior Rambler Club, had an abandoned chicken coop for a clubhouse. I was president, not because I was better but because I was the only one with a T-shirt with "Junior Ramblers" on the front (from the Nash-Rambler car dealership on New York Avenue in Huntington, now the site of Reinwald's Bakery).

On warm summer evenings, most families moved out onto the sun porches to keep cool. Air conditioning was rare then. On hot nights, I moved my bed close to the window and slept with my pillow on the window sill. Many a night I would wake up with a wet pillow and the rain splashing on my face through the screen. The mosquitoes were plentiful. On a hot summer night, you had the choice of sleeping on *top* of the sheets and being eaten alive by a mosquito or roasting with your head *under* the sheets. Sometimes the mosquitoes would bite you right through the sheets. I would wake up in the morning with bumps on my face and body. I have a vivid memory of my father in his shorts, with a rolled newspaper in hand, trying to kill one of those "little monsters."

Around six o'clock every evening, came the familiar jingling bells of the Good Humor Man. At each stop he was surrounded by wide-eyed children with coin in hand, seeking a special treat for the day. I remember Krug's and Dugan's trucks delivering bread to homes, a tradition that appears to be returning. The Carvel stand on New York Avenue opposite Second Street was a favorite place for both children and adults. It was built on the open field that was used by the carnivals that came to town. On the northeast corner of Second Street was Wehr's Grocery Store.

One day in April, 1951, I was walking down the sidewalk in Huntington Station, and loudspeakers from one of the buildings began blasting General Douglas MacArthur's *"Old Soldiers Never Die, They Just Fade Away"* farewell speech to both houses of Congress —an historic moment in the 1950's.

Speaking of the 50's, do you remember *Mad Magazine,* a guy named Alfred E. Neuman and a new product called "TV dinners?" How about the Hula Hoop? Girls used to wear crinolines, petticoats made of a stiff material, worn under a skirt to make it bulge out widely from the waist. They made a swishing sound as they walked down the school halls.

Television didn't take up as much of our time as it does today. A survey recently revealed that the average person watches TV 32 hours a week! Our first set was a black-and-white GE with a 10-inch screen. There was no color TV in those days, and no CNN either. All we had was John Cameron Swayze doing the *Camel News Caravan,* the forerunner of today's news programs. He would "hopscotch the world for headlines" almost every night. He made his program seem like a visit and always ended the news with, "Glad we could get together."

This Ol' House was a song sung by Rosemary Clooney, and not a TV show. We had Howdy Doody, Junior Frolics, The Magic Cottage, Pinhead and Fudini, Kukla, Fran and Ollie, Flash Gordon, Ozzie and Harriet, Father Knows Best, I've Got A Secret, Arthur Godfrey's Talent Scouts, Captain Video and his Video Rangers, I Love Lucy, Dragnet, The Lone Ranger and his faithful Indian companion, Tonto. Tuesday night was Milton Berle's *Texaco Star Theater.*

MOTHBALLS! I don't know anyone today who uses mothballs. Mom would put them everywhere…in basement corners, overstuffed chairs in the parlor (now called a living room or family room) and dresser drawers. When you opened a drawer, they would roll around like tiny marbles. If you put your hand between the pillows of the couch you would find a handful of them.

For our family, Tuesday nights in summer were for going to the movies at the Huntington Station Theater. Good old movies. The themes were simple and nonirritating. Good always triumphed over evil. When leaving a movie I usually felt *good* about something. Most of the violence, if you could call it that, generally occurred off-screen. Today, I look forward to watching American Movie Classics on cable TV. It's relaxing to see movies once again when the wind blows the hair and clothing of the actors in the foreground, but the trees and scenery in the background never moves. (How come, in the old black-and-white cowboy movies, whenever they left the cabin they always walked to the left or right, and never toward the scenery in the background that looked like a painting?) Black-and-white movies seem to go with cowboy and Humphrey Bogart films. Since Ted Turner has colorized some of them, I always remove the color by adjusting my TV set. The movies look better that way. Fake scenery or not, those movies were, and still are, *entertaining.*

Dad and me, 1940's.

After the movie, on our walk back home, we would stop at Reese's Ice Cream Parlor. They had a counter in front with stools, and booths in the back. One of our favorite booths had a large picture of a woman, hat in hand, standing on a windy bluff looking out toward the ocean. Dad would always say she was waiting for her ship to come in. The ice cream was made on the premises in the days before we knew what cholesterol was. By this time I was usually exhausted, and the final walk back home was on the strong shoulders of my father, who would gallop like a horse, to my *"Go faster, Daddy!"*

For children, Saturday afternoons were spent at the Huntington Station Theater. Watching a cowboy movie, we all cheered as the good guys came riding around the pass. Our heroes were Gene Autry (and Champion), Roy Rogers (and Trigger), Red Ryder and Little Beaver, and Hopalong Cassidy. Walter Brennan, and Gabby Hayes were among the few successful stars with no teeth.

There used to be a lady named Mary selling tickets in the hex-shaped booth in front of the theater. Years later, after the movie house was demolished, Mary was selling tickets at the Shore Theater in Huntington. The ticket collector's name was Bill Nolan. I never had to buy a ticket when Bill was on duty. He would let me in for free. I say free, but it really wasn't. In our day, the barter system was alive and well. You did something for someone and they did something to return the favor. My father was always doing, and still does, favors for those who came into his store, and never charged them. His acts of kindness were usually returned, one way or another.

The snows came early in those days. Even then they used to say it was going to be an "old-fashioned winter," meaning it was going to snow a lot. I remember seeing the grey-colored clouds getting ready to puff their tiny flakes. It was always expected to snow all night, and it usually did. I would sit by the kitchen window in the morning, watching the snow fall and listen to the radio, hoping that they would announce that school was closed.

John Hulsen's parents during a very "old-fashioned winter" in the Station, early 1900's.

My father prepared for a major storm as if he were preparing for a war. He would go down into the cellar, dust off the snow shovel and bring up the kerosene lamp. He had plenty of pennies by the fuse box. In the days before circuit breakers, if you ran out of fuses, you could place a penny between the fuse and the electrical connector; this would complete the circuit, but could also overload the wires. We *never* had a flashlight that worked, a tradition that I have kept to this day.

Although Dad was never in the Army, he had an Army jacket with a hood. When he shoveled snow, only his nose stuck out from the hood, followed by billows of white vapor. No matter how deep the snowfall, Dad was what I call a conservative snow remover. The path from our side door to the road was always determined by the width of the snow shovel he used. Sometimes he would walk down the path he had made as if he were balancing on a tightrope. As small as I was, I could touch both sides of the cut in the snow. Conversely, my uncle's driveway was cleaned to the bare ground and wide enough to land a B-22 bomber. As I got older, I began to think my father was right; I noticed that come spring, the snow he didn't remove always seemed to disappear.

I remember Nick LoScalzo delivering ice to the stores on New York Avenue. His truck also delivered coal to our home by sending it down a slide, through the wide open mouth of the cellar window, into our coal bin. The winter job was to constantly feed the belly of the coal stove and remove the ashes. Ashes were either put out for the garbage collection or used to spread on the snow for sure footing.

After we converted from coal to an oil burner, Mom and I chopped up the wooden frame of the coal bin, to enlarge the cellar. But now we had a new worry: losing heat during a power outage. Mom was prepared with her new gas stove; by lighting the oven she could make our kitchen as toasty warm as if we had had a fireplace. And if the lights went out, she would make cupcake-like muffins. Lights out and muffins seemed to go together. Although that was the extent of her baking, it would be tough to match her homemade bread and pizza. Come to think of it, she does make an unbeatable tomato sauce and never uses a recipe.

Parents of Huntington Station children may not have been as well-educated as some people in the "Village," but they were nonetheless determined that their children should receive the best education. School was stressed by our parents as the means to better ourselves. They believed in education, a strong moral tradition, hard work, and that tomorrow would always be a better day. It was just accepted that you did your best in school and you were going to attend college. Parents and teachers gave us hope, courage and determination, so that nothing could stand in the way of our goals in life. When I left high school in 1957, I had a good friend whose father made $12,000 a year. Wow! Mine only made $3,000. I prayed to God, "Please, when I get out of college, if I could only make $12,000 a year." Since then, I've had to ask God for a few raises.

Growing up, I heard about two wars: World War II and the Korean War. My cousin Pat Aurricchio, much older than I, fought in World War II. I remember relatives saying that he was "up front." I couldn't understand at the time that if a war was going on with bullets flying all around, why he would want to be "up front." We have a letter he sent to my father saying, "Love to Uncle Fred, Aunt Lena & Fred Jr. Living in a house right now and just finished eating chicken. P.S. Feeling fine…don't worry. I am somewhere in Germany. The boys and I had one fight so far. Getting ready for another. I didn't get hurt yet." The next day he was killed. I had heard so many things about him, and I'm sorry I never got to know him. Young

Pat Aurricchio

men killed in action will forever stay young while the rest of us grow old. But what a terrible price to pay for staying young.

In the 1950's we had many air raid drills. My father was an air raid warden. The sirens would sound the need for lights out. He would put on his air raid helmet and direct traffic. In school, we had to go in the hallways and sit near the walls with our coats over our heads. In 1961 I married Barbara Joan Albin, and when we bought our first home in 1966, I sent for plans for a home fallout shelter sponsored by the U.S. government. Unfortunately, I never saved the plans I received. Fortunately, we never needed the air raid shelter. Who would have foreseen the breakup of the U.S.S.R. in 1990's?

The town always sponsored fireworks at Manor Field on the 4th of July. I remember the rockets bursting in the summer sky, and the sounds of "ooooh" and "aaaah" as people watched in wonder. How they laughed and cheered. Huntington Manor Fire Department trucks were always present, in case of a spark causing a brush fire. It was such a secure feeling, having those men around. I remember one 4th of July, just as the fireworks started, it began to rain. When the rain got heavy, it was decided to set off all the fireworks in rapid succession. I was sitting on our front porch, watching the crowd making their slow exodus in the driving rainstorm. Fireworks lit up the sky, and each explosion illuminated the grimaces on the faces in the crowd marching up Second Street. It looked like a battle retreat scene from a war movie.

On the corner of Broadway and New York Avenue, we had what was known as the "cop's booth," occupied by one of our local policemen. It was a small building with a desk, chair, telephone, file cabinet and a heater. It also provided us shelter against the cold and rain while we were waiting for the school bus. We also had a jail that was occupied by an occasional drunk.

Businesses were run by people you knew. (I guess someone knew Mr. Macy or Mr. Sears back when they opened their first stores. Not anymore.) Businesses in Huntington Station were named and operated by the people who owned them. We had *Reese's* ice cream, *Hollis* bakery, *Diamond's* and *Popkin's*. In those days, a person's informal surname identified his type of business. We had Freddie *the shoemaker*, Joe *the barber*, Nick *the plumber*, Jimmy *the cop*, and Danny *Ice*. Often we couldn't remember their real last names, but we all knew who we were talking about. Others had nicknames like "Hot Dog," the "Munday brothers," "Flash Gordon," "Violet," "Springer," "Shorty," "Squatty," "Slicky," "Dynamite," "Chicky," "Porky" and "Captain Jim." These names were used with respect and not meant to criticize. If you did something stupid, you were called a "shmoe," in addition to a lot of other names. If you were cranky or unfriendly, you were a "sorehead."

People met daily at neighborhood stores. We didn't have big freezers in those days and our mothers had to shop often. The lack of a means to store food led to people meeting frequently in local stores. This meant that shopping was not a chore, but a social event. The store owners knew you and your family. They worked and lived nearby. Store owners also had another advantage: they were able to serve many generations of the same family.

Today, with our busy schedules, we rarely have time to shop at a local store. It's easier to go to a drive-thru convenience store, call out an order, have the change and order put on the front seat, and speed away. No time to say "hello." We seem to crave impersonal malls, with all the shops stacked on top of each other, sometimes three high. We think it's great to sit in a family room chair and order all sorts of merchandise we don't need, from a television screen, from a person we don't know. To ease our busy-ness we even have an "audio book" that you can "read" while you're driving a car or doing an aerobic workout. All this we are proud to call *progress*, and then have the audacity to complain that people don't care anymore. I hope that someday soon we all can slow down, take a deep breath, and return to the small town values we have lost.

Fred and Lena Sforza, 1990

Whenever I think of Huntington Station, my family and all the people I know and have known, I am reminded of a statement in the novel *Dances with Wolves* by Michael Blake: "I have never met a people more eager to laugh, devoted to family, and dedicated to each other. The only word that comes to mind is harmony."

Note: My conversations with those who wanted to share their memories of Huntington Station has taken me all over Long Island. This section and the following one are in the form of interviews, rather than direct quotations in the first person.

—AVS

BEATRICE TEICH REMEMBERS

Mrs. Beatrice Teich, affectionately called Bea, is the widow of Dr. Samuel Teich. She still lives in their home/office on New York Avenue in Huntington Station. My "one-hour interview" started at nine-thirty and ended at two o'clock; it was difficult to stop reminiscing about life in the Station.

Max and Rosie Teich, Sam's parents, came from Europe and settled in New York City. Max was in a variety of businesses, trying to support his family. He worked in the sweatshops of New York City, as a tailor in Northport, and owned a fruit store in Mineola. Max's brother William raised cows on Park Avenue in Huntington. This may have been an influence for Max to move his family to Huntington Station and establish another business, Teich's Dairy, on Academy Place. Max and Rosie had three children, Samuel, Fannie (Merksamer) and Annie. The death of Annie at an early age was said to be one of the many reasons that compelled Sam to seek a career in medicine.

Sam, born on March 8, 1907, knew hard work. As a child growing up in Huntington Station, he helped his parents deliver milk. The cows grazed in the fields off West Neck Road, the present site of Hillbrae Estates. For many years, neither rain nor snow nor gloom of morning ever stopped this family from their appointed rounds of supplying families with fresh milk.

Like many long-time Huntington Station residents, Sam was educated in our public school system: the Old First School House on School Street, Roosevelt Elementary School, and Huntington High School. Bea told me that Sam had an old Ford that he drove to high school. She said, smiling, "The car did very well downhill, but often had to be pushed uphill."

Most graduates of Huntington High School prior to the 1960's have fond memories of our math teacher, Edna Van Wart. Edna's teaching technique was based mostly on fear. Edna was the kind of teacher that you loved and respected *after* graduation, for the same reasons you disliked her *before* graduation. It's interesting to note that Sam was her student in her first year of teaching and

Howard Teich, Sam's youngest son, was her student in her last year of teaching.

After graduating from Huntington High School, Sam attended Cornell University, where he received his bachelor's degree. He earned his medical degree from Long Island College of Medicine, followed by an internship at Coney Island Hospital in Brooklyn.

While going to school, Sam commuted on the Long Island Railroad. One day while riding the train, he noticed a beautiful young woman sitting in a seat near him. Beatrice Katzenbogen was talking to a girlfriend about her relatives who lived in Huntington. She had no idea that Sam was listening to the entire conversation. Sam, too shy at the time to introduce himself, was impressed enough to go home and tell his mother that he would someday marry this young woman, whose name he didn't even know yet.

Beatrice Katzenbogen was born in Brooklyn on October 12, 1910. After moving to many parts of the country, the family settled in Babylon. Bea had a job in New York City and traveled the Long Island Railroad. Coming back from work, she had to change trains at Jamaica, and it was on the first leg of this trip that Sam had seen, listened to and fallen in love with her. At the time, Bea was unaware of Sam's existence. His shyness kept them from meeting the first time, but fate caused them to meet again much later.

At a dance in Massapequa in 1932, Sam was introduced to Bea. He instantly recognized her as the young woman he had seen on the train. Since she had helped to organize the dance, she was responsible for speaking to each person as they were leaving, asking them if they had a good time and if they would come to another dance that her temple was having the following week. When she asked Sam, he said, "Sure, if you'll dance with me." When she said yes, his shyness overpowered him again and suddenly he said he couldn't make it because he had to work. However, as they talked they discovered that their relatives knew each other, and they agreed to meet in front of the information booth of the Long Island Railroad Station in New York and have dinner at a Chinese restaurant in Brooklyn. After dating for the next three years, they were married on December 15, 1935.

Samuel and Beatrice Teich, 1960s.

When Sam had started his medical practice in Huntington Station in 1933, his office was above the stores on 1189 New York Avenue (Horne Paint & Dave's Stationery Stores). He and Bea lived for a while on New York Avenue between 9th and 10th streets. In March 1940 they moved into their newly built home at 1090 New York Avenue, opposite School Street.

Married for almost sixty years, they had three sons, Morton (a physician in immunology), Stephen (a physician in forensic psychology), and Howard (a lawyer). All three sons practice their professions and live in New York City. Sam and Bea have six grandchildren, Aaron, Alyson, Sean, Karina, David and Marko.

Howard, Stephen and Morton Teich, 1960's.

Bea remembered that one night after they were engaged, they were at a hospital dance with a good friend, Dr. Morris Milstein, a Huntington Station dentist. Sam, called out on an emergency, asked Morris to take care of his girlfriend until he returned. When Sam came back, he laughingly told Morris that this *medical* emergency was really a *dental* emergency, and not only that — it was Morris's patient. Sam, the typical country doctor, was capable of handling all kinds of emergencies.

Sam was the first physician to be drafted from Huntington Station. Captain Samuel Teich began his army career in August 1942. While he was stationed in Texas, Bea, the ever-faithful companion, made several trips to visit him, often searching the training fields to find him. While he was stationed in the States, Bea and the boys lived close to the camp to be near him. I asked her about the mortgage on their new home when Sam was drafted, and she explained that the early 1940's were tough, not only for her family but for all families whose husbands went off to fight. I could see that it was her determination that resulted in the preservation of their home.Nevertheless, Bea would only say that she was grateful for the moral support from friends and relatives during this stressful time in her life.

Following are excerpts from a letter Sam sent to *The Long Islander,* published in the September 17th 1942 edition under the headline "First Lieut. S. Teich Writes From Camp:"

To the Editor of the Long Islander
Dear Sir:

During the past week, I have received my first copy of your paper and I assure you it was most welcome.

A month ago today, I left Huntington to report to my regiment at Camp Bowie, Texas…I was sent out to catch up with the regiment which was on maneuvers in Louisiana. Since I arrived in this State, I have been…wandering about in the woodlands, living regular hours, eating good food, staying out in the fresh air 24 hours a day.

In this life, which might almost be an ideal vacation, we miss one important element…home. We miss our family and friends and the life we knew…we did not realize how much they were a part of us until after we left. Our only contacts with home are through letters from family and friends and through local newspapers. The arrival of the mail is the most important time of the day; we are cheered when we get some but depressed when we get none.

I want to again thank you for your paper… Through you I would like to thank all the friends in town who have been so decent to me and my family…

Sincerely yours,
Samuel Teich 1st Liet. M.C.

I can just see Sam sitting on his bunk, writing these words to his hometown paper. It shows the value to our boys in the army of letters from family and friends and a newspaper from home. Many of them had never been away from home before. News about his hometown must have been heartwarming to Sam. His letter reveals a sensitive person, with strong family values. The small-town life he enjoyed had been disrupted. He missed his wife Bea, his children, family and friends. Nevertheless, he was in the service of his country and he was going to do the best job he could. He was not critical of being drafted, only appreciative of the family and friends he loved and had to leave behind.

Captain Samuel Teich

Captain Sam was a platoon leader in combat from June 1944 to April 1945. As a member of the 609th Medical Company, he was awarded the Bronze Star for meritorious service. He was praised for ensuring that his platoon "performed all assigned tasks in a superior manner," overcame "all problems presented to him by excellent knowledge and adaptability," and "rendered excellent service under all variations of difficulties." I couldn't help thinking that these were the same characteristics that made Sam the outstanding country doctor of Huntington Station in his private life. Sam was committed to all his patients and knew no color barriers — truly a man ahead of his time. His medical unit was among the first to treat victims of the Holocaust. Sam shot many rolls of film, at the camps and of the prisoners, that have never been developed. Although there is little hope that developing them today would produce any usable photographs, Bea expressed a desire to try.

Sam was a true country doctor, seeing many patients during the day and going on house calls in the evening. He would treat all forms of illnesses. As Bea said, "Today, you have to have a doctor for the right eye and one for the left eye!" Bea was very often Sam's chauffeur on his house calls. She would drive, and between house calls Sam would try to sleep; sometimes he would get as little as two hours a night. He could never be assured of a day off. They could be on their way to an affair in the city when an emergency signal from his beeper would turn them back towards Huntington Station. Once, Bea recalled, Sam examined a young boy at home and diagnosed appendicitis. He put the child into his car and brought him to the hospital himself. Bea, his constant companion, said she feels that over the years she earned at least half a medical degree. I think she deserves a degree because she was just as devoted to medicine and patients as was Dr. Sam.

Sam and Bea Teich, 1993.

Knowing what it is to maintain a dental practice, with all the emergencies, I asked Bea whether Dr. Sam ever got discouraged about being always on call. "Never," was her reply. "We treated all the babies as if they were our own children. " Often, after office hours, Sam would stop by at a relative's home, knowing they didn't feel well, just to see how they were doing.

Sam died in December 1995, closing the final chapter in the book of small town medical practices. I have the feeling that if he had to start a medical practice in our present environment, he would still be our Dr. Sam, although I do know he'd be disappointed in the way we must run our practiccs today.

I asked Bea, "When you could have lived anywhere in the township of Huntington, why did you choose to stay in Huntington Station?" Her reply was quick and simple: "Why not? He lived in Huntington Station all his life. After we married, this was our home and this was our town."

"What would you want everyone to know about you and Dr. Sam?" was my concluding question. "I want them to know that we were a very close couple," she said. "We had a wonderful and meaningful family life. Our home was always open to everyone. They knew, no matter what time it was, if our living room light was on they could come in."

The Teich home and office.

Thank you, Bea, for being his constant companion and for being a part of the history of our community. Keep the living room light on, for we won't say goodbye to Dr. Sam, we'll just say, *see you later!*

Eleanor Reed gave a beautiful eulogy at Dr. Sam's funeral:

"I met him in the early 60's. Dr. Teich was a warm, quiet and kind person. He was a friend to all mankind. Dr. Sam had a good sense of humor and was always willing to help you, whether it was medical, financial or just an encouraging word. He was there whenever you needed him.

"Dr. Teich was truly one of God's instruments. Twice, I had a close call with death and he was there with his skillful mind and hands to touch me and make me well again.

"In helping to care for Dr. Teich in the last few years, I noticed that his gait was a lot slower and he didn't converse often, but he had a smile that would brighten up the darkest day.

"Now, God has called him from labor to reward. We are going to miss him… it is time for him to rest. We love him. But God loves him best."

JUNE HESS KELLY REMEMBERS

One of the great pleasures of writing about history is coming into contact with people that you have never known and leaving with the feeling that you have known them all your life. This interview was one of those instances. My first contact with the Hess family was a telephone conversation with June Hess Kelly's grandson, James. James takes care of his grandmother and not only invited me into their home but also found all the photographs of the H. Bellas Hess Estate that appear in this section. James was also an important factor in enabling me to complete a missing section of Huntington Station's history.

Interviewing June Kelly took me out to East Hampton. The main road leading to her present home reminded me of the entrance to her family home in Huntington Station. The entrance to the Hess estate was from New York Avenue. The home was well protected by woods so that no one could see the house from the road. Huge iron gates guarded a picturesque tree-lined driveway winding south to the entrance. The uppermost branches of the trees joined together, creating a tunnel-like appearance. I have driven to the Hamptons many times, but this was the first time I noticed that the trees lining both sides of the road arched over it in the same way. Now, whenever I travel on this part of the road to Montauk, I will always think of June Kelly.

I can still remember walking home with my friends from a movie in the village and passing by the entrance to the Hess estate, part of which is now the site of Huntington High School and the Big H shopping center. It was a "double dare" to see how far you could run down this dark corridor of a driveway. Even on a "triple dog dare," the ultimate of all dares, I was never able to make it all the way down the driveway to see the house.

My interview with June Kelly was a pleasant look into Huntington Station's past and a short story of her life with what she said were "over-protective" but loving and caring parents. The many hours I spent with June Kelly went quickly. Her patience with my questions was unbelievable, and it was remarkable how much she remembered about the town, her home, and the part of her life she spent in Huntington Station. James helped too, by prompting her to "tell him the story about…!"

Harry Bellas Hess was born in Iowa. As a young man, an idea came to him when he ordered a gun from a newspaper advertisement. When the gun arrived in the mail a few weeks later, he thought that it would be a great idea to have a catalog from which people could order and receive many kinds of goods by mail without leaving home. This new concept would be especially useful for people in remote areas. It made big city shopping as close to them as the catalog on their kitchen table.

After leaving Iowa, he worked for a while for a dry goods company in St. Louis. The company did not have a very large mail order business and H.B.H. did his best to convince them to enlarge their catalog operations. H.B.H. then moved onto Chicago. While he and a friend were standing outside a window of the Chicago Beach Hotel watching a dance going on inside, his eyes focused on one beautiful young girl in a pink dress with a "rose stuck in her puffy sleeve." H.B.H. told his friend, "That is the girl I am going to marry."

He and Mabel Bingham did indeed marry, and had a daughter whom they named June. They came to New York City and he started his own catalog business. National Bellas Hess became one of the largest mail order catalog businesses in the United States. The company later merged with a firm in Brooklyn, and just before 1929 H.B.H. sold the catalog business to Sears & Roebuck.

H. Bellas and Mabel Hess, 1920's.

Although H.B.H. had his business and home in New York City, he wanted his daughter to experience the country life. In the early part of this century he chose Huntington Station as the place for his family to have a weekend and summer home. Since he would have to commute to his business in New York City, he wanted property close to the railroad station. The land he chose was about halfway between the station and the village.

"Originally there was a white farmhouse on the property," June recalled. "It was a really beautiful one on the top of a hill." This hill, according to June, was the "second highest to Janes Hill. We could see the sailboats in the harbor." H.B.H. eventually bought the surrounding properties so that no one could build around him. Later he purchased the "old farm house on McKay Road with a pond in the front. It had a huge red barn. The people who owned the farm before raised ducks. Our gardener lived in the house with his family." The Hess estate eventually encompassed about 150 acres and bordered New York Avenue, Oakwood Road and McKay Road.

H.B.H. had a friend in Connecticut who had designed an Italian-style home, and he was intrigued with this architectural style. He had the old farm house torn down, and built a "very formal, Italian-style stucco house with a tile roof and a terrace out front. A vista in front of the home was planted with cedars on each side. As you came up the driveway you had a beautiful view of the cedar trees." June explained that this was why they referred to their home as The Cedars. "The house was built with materials imported from Italy. A lot of work and a lot of love went in to the making of our home."

A Pictorial Guide to the H. Bellas Hess Estate

Front view. A picturesque tree-lined driveway began at New York Avenue. About 500 feet into the estate, it curved to the right and proceeded through stately cedar trees to the front of the mansion.

East wall. The driveway continued, curving around this wall on the left side of the house and leading to the entrance at the back. The staircase in the foreground was the service entrance to the kitchen.

Entrance gate. The gates of this archway provided a panoramic view of the back of the estate. The path to the right led to the front wall gate seen in the photo on the previous page.

Rear view. The back of the mansion, just inside the main entrance gate. The circular driveway welcomed guests to the port cochere or the main entrance. In the foreground is the path to the front wall gate.

Port cochere. The gateway projecting over the driveway was the guest entrance to the home.

Stable and garage. In this photo, two horses — Tango and Dixie — are in their stalls.

The main entrance, from the port cochere. A spacious marble center hall extended to a circular area at the front, which had three doors leading to the terrace. The dining room was to the right of this hall, the living room to the left.

The dining room. The door behind the screen led to the kitchen. One step up from the dining room was the library, or den, which had a fireplace flanked by benches and a locked gun closet. The window overlooked the front terrace.

View from the dining room through the center hall, to the living room. The main entrance at the back of the house was just to the left, in the center hall.

The living room. The window in front overlooked the terrace. The living room had an entrance to an enclosed patio on the side of the house. Above this patio was an open patio off the master bedroom, providing a wide view of the Huntington Village area.

A view from the terrace, looking towards Huntington Village. Because of the high elevation, sailboats could be seen in the harbor.

Front view. The circular area had three doors leading to the terrace. June Hess Kelly's bedroom immediately above had a commanding view of the village area.

June Hess Kelly had many memories of events during her childhood in Huntington Station. One time her father, knowing that she wanted a pony, brought home what he called a "donkey pony." The donkey was in the back seat of the family limousine with its tail out one window and its nose out the other. It must have been some sight driving down New York Avenue. She laughed as she remembered harnessing the donkey to a four-seater straw cart and the fun she had driving around the estate.

"There were bobsled races on Main Street, every winter," she recalled. "The sleds came down Lawrence Hill Road and Main Street and into town. As a youngster, I watched as they came down the hill. The races were fast and scary.

"There was a movie house opposite the Huntington Hotel (the present site of Aboff's). Father would take me to see a movie, which was a great thrill.

"The Trade School on Main Street in Huntington had a dancing school which I attended and thoroughly enjoyed. I was about ten years old then. I remember one time wearing a new blue velvet dress with beautiful embroidery on the front. My mother came to the class early to pick me up, which was an unusual thing for her to do. I was very upset and didn't know why I had to leave, since I was having such a good time. Mother said, "Your instructor is very understanding and kind. We are taking you out of class today for a very special reason. Someday you will realize why it is so important." It seems that Enrico Caruso was singing at the Metropolitan Opera in New York City that afternoon, and both my mother and my instructor agreed that it would be a great experience for me to see him in person. I think he died soon after that appearance."

(Enrico Caruso (1873-1921) the great Italian tenor, had one of the most brilliant voices in the history of music. Caruso's success was almost unparalleled. He made his last appearance at the Metropolitan Opera in *La Juive* on December 24, 1920. June's mother's decision gave her the opportunity to see a living legend just before he died.)

"I had always wondered what it would be like to sleigh ride down our driveway to New York Avenue and then down the hill to Main Street in Huntington Village, to see how far I could go. After one big snow storm, I got on my American Flexible Flyer sled and, without anyone knowing I was going, started downhill on my quest to reach the village. My thrilling ride took me well past Main Street. I did have to walk back, but my mission was accomplished!

"My mother was a Huntington Red Cross Teacher. She had taken a nursing course and felt that children should be aware of World War II. We had a large center hall in our home with a table in the middle where she taught children how to roll bandages for the war effort. She took the bandages to the army camps in Smithtown and Yaphank.

"We had horses, and rode frequently. One time Mother was knocked off her horse. We were coming back from a drag hunt and trying to cross New York Avenue to the entrance to our driveway. A motorcycle came down a curve in the road and both my mother and the cyclist, in an attempt to avoid one another, collided at our driveway entrance. Mother fell to the ground, injuring her face on the gravel. The horse ended up on his back, but got up and ran towards the village.

Mabel Hess and the Red Cross children.

"Although my father felt sorry for my mother, he was also a little provoked, and said to me, 'Your mother will never learn. I've told her many times to turn the horse in the *direction* of the sound and not *away* from it.' Mother gave up riding and we never went on a hunt again. I was very disappointed, because I was quite a rider for my age. I had learned well from my father.

"I missed the hurdles we had jumped during the hunt. We had many riding trails on our property, and one day I decided to build my own hurdle in a wooded area that I thought was ideal. I knew no one would ever find it. It was a wonderful job, if I may say so myself. I could go off on my horse alone, not tell anyone where I was going, and jump as much as I wanted to. This was the most emancipated thing I had ever done. I was about 11 years old.

"Years later, after I was married, I was having lunch with my father in a hotel in New York, which we often did. He said, 'You know something? I have never spoken to you about this before, but I want to give you four marks, the highest you can get, for that wonderful hurdle you built in the woods.' I gasped. I couldn't believe my ears. 'You mean to tell me that you knew all the time that the hurdle was there? Why didn't you say anything?' His reply was typical for any father in a strong father-daughter relationship. 'I knew you had made it and I was very proud of you. I didn't want your mother to know it was there. She would have had twenty thousand fits and stopped it, because you know she never rode again after the accident. Knowing what jumping meant to you, it would have all been spoiled for you, and I didn't want that to happen.'"

(I've left my favorite June Kelly story for last. I think it's a perfect example of how, rich or poor, there is a special relationship between a father and his children — wanting them to be free to choose, but also to protect them.)

"During World War I my father was in the Secret Service. As he was stationed on Long Island, we spent more time together at our home in Huntington Station. During this period, I went to grade school on Main Street in Huntington.

"Our chauffeur drove me to school every morning and dropped me off. This embarrassed me and made me feel like an oddball. I told my father, 'I want to go to school like everyone else.' Father asked me, 'Well, how do all the other children go to school?' 'Why, they ride their bicycles,' was my reply. 'You mean to tell me that you want to take that long trip every morning and every afternoon?' 'Oh, yes,' I said quickly. Father thought it over and said, 'I went to school on my bicycle, so I don't see why you shouldn't.' I was so thrilled, and felt emancipated.

"The next morning I woke up early, very excited and ready to ride to school on my bicycle. Lo and behold, Father had the chauffeur come along on *his* bicycle. I couldn't believe it. Having the chauffeur there spoiled everything. You must remember that my parents had only one child, and I was very sheltered. But I made such a big fuss over the incident that I finally got a chance to go alone on my bicycle to school."

Thank you, June Hess Kelly, for your unique memories of Huntington Station. I will never forget you.

Postcript:

In the March 25, 1954 issue of *The Long Islander* it was announced that builders had contracted to buy the beautiful Bellas Hess estate. Plans were made to develop the area with stores and garden apartments. The builders applied for a change of zone, and to make the deal even sweeter they offered the Town of Huntington the Hess residence with "suitable adjoining property" for parking, to be used as the new Town Hall. The Town Board turned down the offer.

The mansion burning in 1958.

The beautiful residence disappeared forever from the history of Huntington Station when it caught fire in 1958. Although the structure was destroyed, the love that went into making it a home endures, and at least some of its memories are now preserved for future generations.

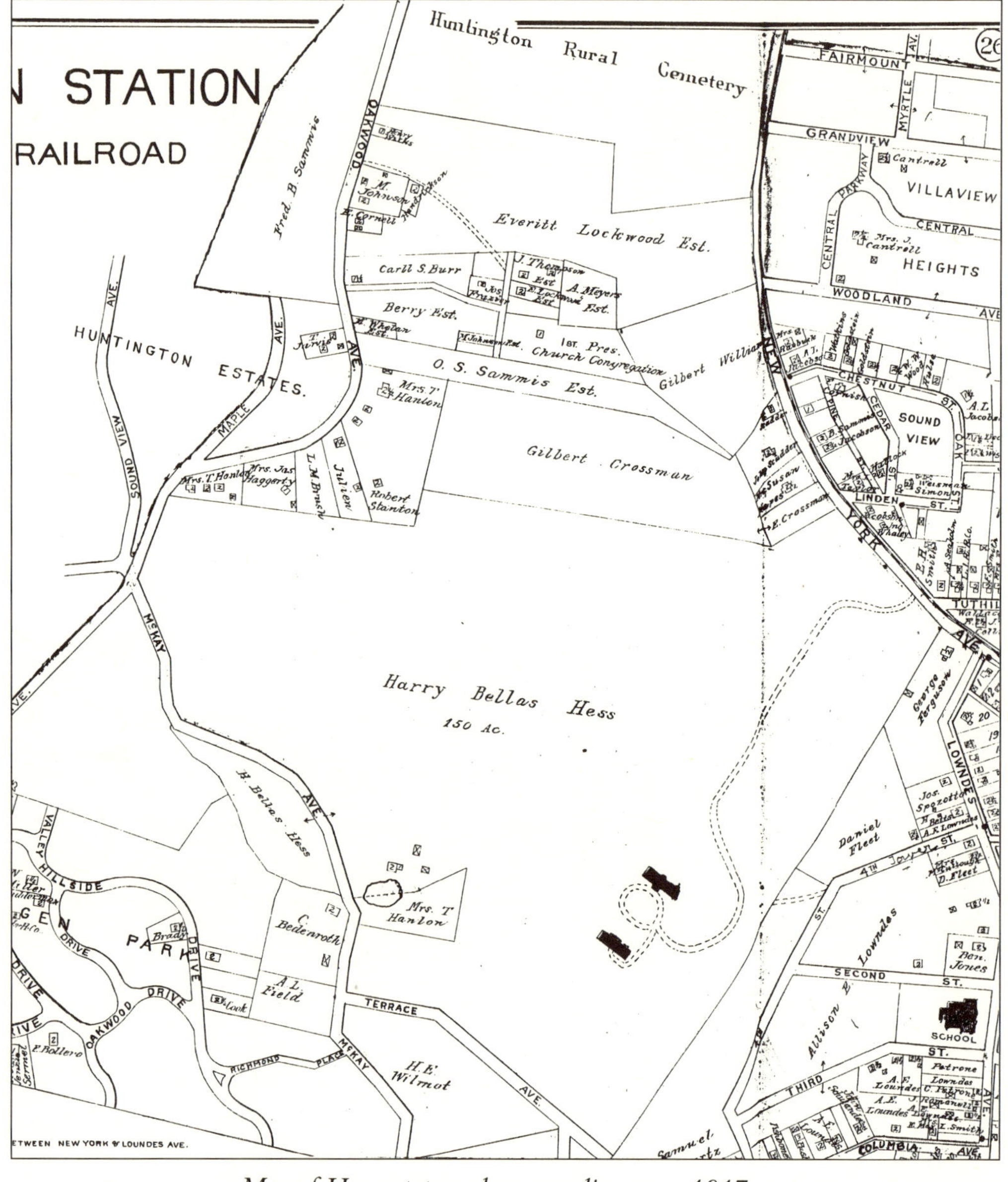

Map of Hess estate and surrounding area, 1917.

PART III

IMAGES OF OUR TOWN

Aerial view, 1955: New York Avenue at right, running north/south; railroad tracks at 45° angle, running from bottom center to right edge of photo. Large open area in center of photo is the Hess estate.

Approximately the same view, 1996.

The aerial photograph on page 134 was taken in 1955, and shows the H. Bellas Hess estate in the center; the light rectangles are land that was being farmed on the estate. The Long Island Railroad tracks cut in at a 45-degree angle at the bottom of the picture. The wide white road at the right, running approximately north/south, is New York Avenue.

The aerial photo on page 135 — taken in 1996 — shows the same area at present. Huntington High School and the Big H Shopping Center take up a part of the Hess estate, and the rest has been subdivided for homes. Note that the area around the train station has changed completely; a large parking garage and many parking lots have replaced the numerous stores, and some houses, that used to be there.

The photograph below, taken in the 1950's, shows how the area appeared before urban renewal. The view is eastward. Roosevelt Elementary School is in the center, with Winding Street to the south (right), School Street to the north (left), and Lowndes Avenue, somewhat obscured by trees, to the east. The map on the opposite page will be helpful for orientation.

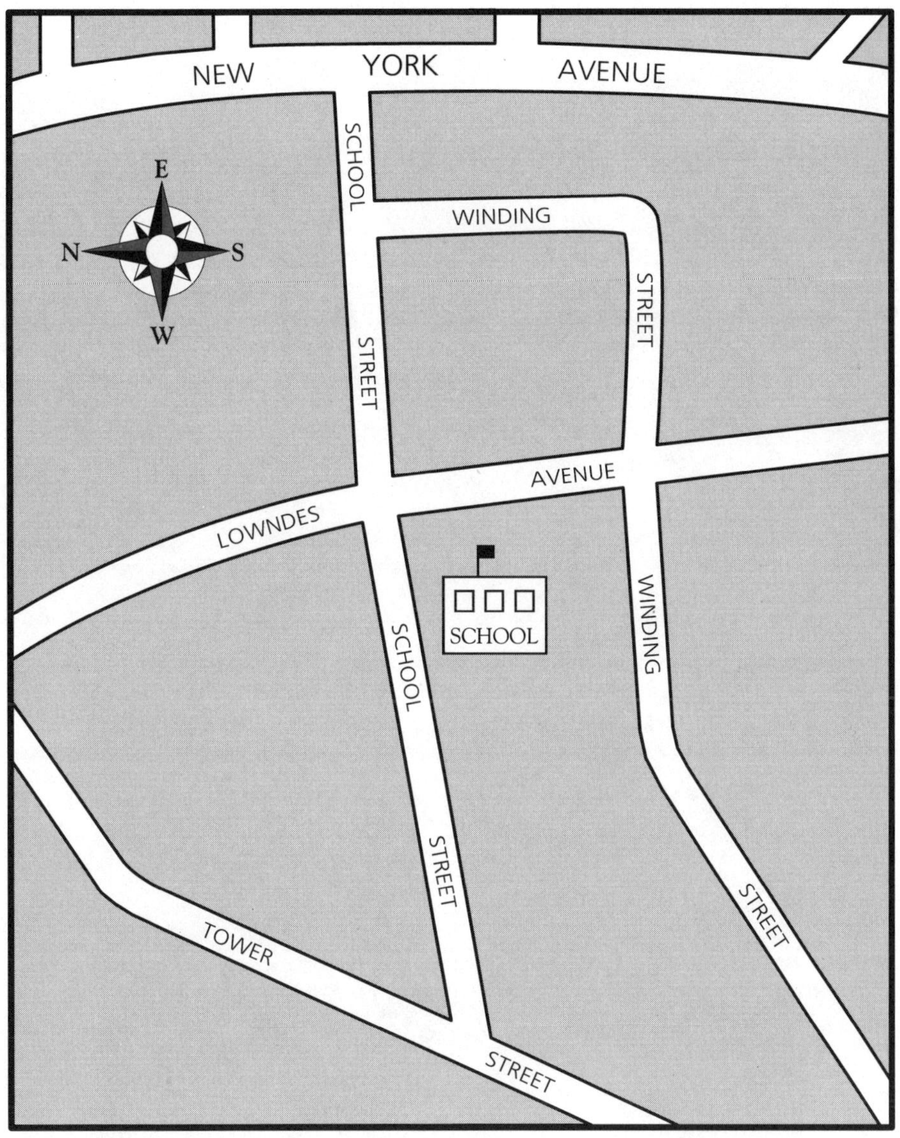
NEW
YORK
AVENUE
SCHOOL
STREET
WINDING
STREET
E
N
S
W
AVENUE
LOWNDES
SCHOOL
SCHOOL
STREET
WINDING
STREET
TOWER
STREET

The following photographs from the 1930's to the 1960's (before urban renewal) provide more detailed images of the many changes over the years.

Broadway (called Lincoln Avenue in the early 1900's), with trolley tracks in the 1930's. Stores: pharmacy, Romano's Bakery, Hugh P. Arthur Real Estate, Insurance, A&P, meat store, garage.

Broadway, 1935: garage, restaurant (formerly the Post Office), drug store and billiard parlor.

Broadway, 1935: Steuben Bar & Grill, with Nick Bros. Coal, Wood and Ice truek in front.

North side of Broadway, viewed from railroad station. Last building on right is the Long Island Herald. *Building behind it is livery stable.*

Between Broadway and Galliene Place: Crystal Market, Campus Restaurant ("Always open, tables for ladies, Sunday dinner 85¢"), August Barber Shop ("Shave 40¢, Ladies and Children's haircut, 20¢").

Huntington Station Post Office (at right) was later occupied by Harwein Hardware.

Liquor store on corner of Galienne Place and New York Avenue, 1941. Tall man in middle is Jack Earle, a liquor salesman considered at the time to be "the tallest man in the world."

The photographs that follow were taken on New York Avenue from Lowndes Avenue to Columbia Place from the 1930's through the 1960's.

Candy and soda shop in 1935: later Reese's Ice Cream Parlor, later Joost's; at right, Diamond's Department Store.

Larkhart Lincoln Mercury, at the corner of Lowndes Avenue and New York Avenue, 1950's. Building behind is the Post Office.

1960's: Boyle's Diner, Mr. Rotella the tailor, Al's Variety Surplus Store (former site of Pettit and Son).

1935, New York Avenue between Columbia Place and School Street, showing A&P and Axelrod's, both of which would become Ben Franklin 5&10.

1960's: Columbia Hall at corner of Columbia Place (the alleyway); the hall had bowling in rear of building, Silberfein Dress Shop on 2nd floor, and basketball court on top floor. First floor was originally Hulsen's Stationery, then Popkin's, and later L.I. Paneling Centers.

These photographs from 1935 are of New York Avenue, from School Street to Church Street.

Huntington Manor Fire Department, Rubin's Cleaner (tailor), Louis Fruit & Vegetables, Sarrow's Grocery.

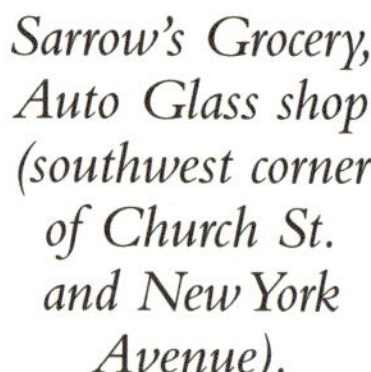

Sarrow's Grocery, Auto Glass shop (southwest corner of Church St. and New York Avenue).

Nat's Men Clothes, A.B. Gross Auto Accessories, Halpern Stationery, North Shore Paper Company (northwest corner of Church St. and New York Avenue).

EPILOG

Here we are at the end of the trip back to our small community in Huntington Station. I hope you enjoyed reliving some of the story of the town that used to be. We certainly have seen many changes in the Town of Huntington over the years. Acres of farmland have been transformed into housing developments; most of our potato and corn fields have disappeared; huge hotels are rising up in areas we once considered remote, and mom-and-pop businesses are struggling with competition from malls and superstores. I consider myself fortunate to have known Huntington Station when it was "country."

While writing this book, I drove through the Station area several times, and almost expected to see the old buildings and people again. But the dreary parking lots quickly brought me back to reality. Nonetheless, I feel the satisfaction of knowing that I have documented a portion of our history.

This trip into the past provided me with a kind of release from today's pressures. Were times really simpler then? I am certain that they were. When I was young, I was invincible. My worries were few. Remember how simple life used to be? It was simple because *somebody else was in charge of worry*. They had to worry about running a business and whether or not tomorrow the bottom might drop out. They had to worry about the mortgage, paying the monthly bills, federal, state and local taxes, and real estate taxes. Taxes if you made money, and taxes if you spent money. In the end, to give you a good send-off, they taxed your estate and your funeral. Someone else had to worry about the health of parents, children, and relatives. Another person was in charge of buying a car, shopping for food, and putting the garbage out. I didn't have to be concerned about the state of the economy, whether or not the stock market was up or down, international affairs, terrorism, or if some deranged person would start a world war. I didn't have to worry about having enough money to retire, or how much longer I would live. Remember, I was invincible — I was going to live forever. But would I want to go back? Certainly not! All I asked for was a break in the action. I got that by writing this book and thinking about simpler times. Now I'm ready to be in charge of worry again.

Organizing the stories, researching the history and grouping the photographs proved to be more arduous than I anticipated. At times I became a little discouraged trying to organize the final manuscript. But the enthusiasm of the people

I interviewed, and the expressions on the faces of each person I spoke to at my lectures on "Do You Remember Freddie's Shoe Repair?" was all the inspiration I needed to continue my task.

The obligation of the present is to preserve the past for future generations. In a small way, this book is my attempt to do so. It is hardly a complete story. Other people are needed to contribute their memories and photographs, to add to the history of our small town. I have only scratched the surface, but at least it is a beginning.

REMEMBER HOW SIMPLE LIFE USED TO BE?

Well, it could be simple again. All we need is time. Life is *all about time.*

We created the idea of time so we could have some control and order in our lives. Time is constant, but it seems to change from minute to minute, day to day, person to person. Even our moods can change our concept of time. The busier we get, the more time becomes a very precious, elusive thing.

We spend a good part our lives trying to *organize our time.* Although we have *all the time* there is, we always feel we need *more time.* Most often we find that we have *no time.*

There is no way to *save time.* We cannot predict *future time***.** We can't go back to the past and *redo time.* Money can't *buy time.* When we see how quickly time disappears, we often wish we could *stop time,* but time stops for no one.

Moods change time. How remarkable that when we are having a *good time* we feel that *time flies.* Conversely, *bad time*s time are perceived as *slow time.* On occasion we look for *time to kill* or *time to just do nothing.* We have songs about a *time to live,* a *time to die,* and a *time to love.*

Young people are accused of *wasting their time.* In my youth, summer vacation days were endless. What did we care about time? We were going to live forever. By my teen years I was busy attending college, but at least I had *some time.* Later, starting my profession, I was lucky to have *any time.* Days began passing by at a blurring speed. Months and years were blending together.

Time slowly takes away our youth. We think we have *all the time in the world* until one day we wake up and realize we're older; we have children and grandchildren, and *time is growing short.* When I saw my hair turning gray, *Father Time* took on a new meaning. Losing a good friend to cancer, and having my closest relatives dying, I have a feeling that I am *running out of time.* Age, on the other hand, has *given me time* to have experiences I couldn't have had as a youth. I've seen our children mature and our grandchildren grow. Having grandchildren is seeing one's own children growing up all over again — memories of *happy times.*

Time is the accumulation of experience within the span we call our *lifetime,* which prepares us for eternity. When we compare our lifetime to all the lives in eternity, our portion is only a small fragment. Small but not insignificant. All of us, in our time, provide a link for eternity. That makes each of us important.

I have made a vow to *enjoy time,* and just remember what I called my youth. With my *present time,* I will do my best to be kind to myself and to others and *make more time* to spend with those who mean the most to me. I will *take the time* to say to them, "I love you."

THE DESTRUCTION OF A SMALL TOWN

The events and experiences of the people I interviewed, although unique to these individuals, could happen anywhere in the United States. It could be AnySmallTown, U.S.A. How was it possible to destroy a town and leave no sign of it behind? This was not a war — they called it "progress." The destruction of our town not only had an *emotional effect* on the people who lived there, but has an impact on future generations. Those who lived there have had a part of their identity removed. The newcomers have no town to identify with. What can we do in the future to prevent this from happening elsewhere? We are here not to just witness events; we must do something to shape their outcome.

I am concerned for the future of Huntington Village. It has a wealth of historical buildings. But what do you see on Main Street today? Many stores are vacant, and businesses that have been here for generations are closing their doors — Knight's, Lyons, June Peters, just to name a few. Is there life after the malls and superstores? They offer big discounts and plenty of parking and that's all. They lack the closeness that we have in hometown stores.

I valued the relationships we had with storekeepers in Huntington Station. Many stores in the Village maintain that personal service and warmth. So do we run to the chain stores to buy our office supplies, or shop locally? It's up to us to make sure Huntington Village stays vibrant.

It's hard for small stores to compete with big stores, not only in price but also in *parking.* Does the Town of Huntington really make that much money on the parking meters, or does the money just cover the salaries to maintain the meters and collect the coins? In this age of plastic money, people rarely carry the coins needed to feed these little demons. Having to run into the bank to make a deposit, and finding a parking ticket on your windshield when you return is not the way to charm people to come to Huntington Village.

In order to survive, many Long Island communities, including Huntington, have created business improvement districts (BIDS) to improve their downtown commercial areas. They are merchants and officials teaming up to give the town a facelift. If the Village is going to get its fair share of business, it will have to find ways to compete. Other towns have survived with local support, and it can survive too! Downtown Huntington Village must not become another downtown Huntington Station.

I REMEMBER HUNTINGTON STATION...

Broadway, before: B&B Market, Recreation (pool) hall, Lukralle Bros. Furniture.

Broadway, after: Just a parking lot.

Corner of Broadway and New York Avenue, 1930's. The bank, the stores and the depot "anchored" the town and provided a sense of security.

Same corner in 1996; everything was swept away for parking lots.

1960's, looking north on New York Avenue. Urban renewal had already started destruction.

Same view, 1995: The wind blows over the parking lots.

A RETURN TO VALUES

Huntington Station still represents the melting pot that all of America claims to be. Its people still are a wide range of ethnic groups trying to make a better quality of life for themselves and for their children. Writing this book has given me an appreciation of the family values of the past and has made me reevaluate our values today. I have a better appreciation of what it means to be a son, a husband, a father, and now a grandfather.

Newt Gingrich, in the "Contract With America," spoke about *a return to values.* I like that phrase. In old Huntington Station, we had certain values that today we tend to forget, or perhaps put aside, as we make our way through the weeds of life. I mean the values of *respect, discipline, religious faith, self-sacrifice and personal responsibility.* In 1992, Vice President Dan Quayle gave a speech to the Commonwealth Club of California that has since been known as the "Murphy Brown Speech." He stated that family values, and two parents married to each other, should be considered the ideal for raising children. This set off a vigorous debate across America. Today, many admit that there were good things in his speech; even *The Atlantic* published a cover story titled, "Dan Quayle Was Right."

Over the years, we went from *Father Knows Best* with Robert Young, to *Life without a father* in Murphy Brown. Once upon a time, in family life, there was a mother and a father, each with distinct roles. Fathers typically were the sole economic providers, the authority figures and the technical advisors. Mothers took care of the home and children. Today these roles have blurred; by desire or necessity, either sex has become the economic provider or primary child raiser — and sometimes both. The crucial point, regardless of which role is taken by each parent, is that children need the role models and the responsibility of *both* a mother *and* a father. We need our family structure to survive as a society.

Although not perfect, America still gives us the opportunity to be successful. And family values give us the strength to improve ourselves. As you read this book, I hope you recognized the family values directly or indirectly implied in all my interviews. These values played an important part in making Huntington Station a great town to live in.

Granted, we had fewer people than we do today, and they knew each other. We had a sense of community, and *harmony.* I don't want to create the impression that people were singing and dancing in the streets every day, because it wasn't that way. But we were all concerned about the well-being of our community, and we helped by responding to the problems. When people understand the needs of their town, it becomes obvious that they must get together, organize and change things for the better.

I hope that as we approach the 21st century, the movement that started a return to our values doesn't die. Let's make a pledge to return to our small town values — the kind we had in Huntington Station. The kind of values that made America great.

BIBLIOGRAPHY

Coles, Robert R., *The Long Island Indian.* New York, 1911: Little, Brown & Company

Jackson, Birdsall, *How They Lived.* Rockville Center, NY, 1941: Paumerok Publishers.

Lott, Roy, *Huntington Tap Roots.* 1960, Town of Huntington, N.Y.

Marshall, Bernice, *The Rest of the Story, 1929-1961.* New York, 1963: Ira J. Friedman

McDermott, Charles J., *Suffolk County.* New York, 1965: James H. Heineman, Inc.

Overton, Jacqueline, *Long Island's Story,* New York, 1963: Ira J. Friedman

Street, Charles R., *Huntington Town Records.* 1889, Town of Huntington, N.Y.

Tooker, William Wallace, *Indian Place-names on Long Island.* New York, 1962: Ira J. Friedman

Town of Huntington, *Our Town, Huntington 1653-1953.* Huntington Tercentenary, Inc.

Ziel, Ron and Foster, George, *Steel Rails to The Sunrise.* New York, 1965: Duell, Sloan & Pearce

Statistics on fire prevention and control, the movies, and leeches: *The Academic American Encyclopedia,* Grolier Electronic Publishing, 1995 (Prodigy).

PHOTO CREDITS

Front cover: Huntington Historical Society. Back cover, left: Huntington Historical Society, right, the author.

P. 19, top, Ron Ziel Collection; pp. 20-23, Ron Ziel Collection; p. 29, top, John Hulsen; p. 47, Fred Ulmer; pp. 49-50, the Mohlenhoff family; pp. 53-54; Ray Devine; p. 79, top, the Jacobsen family; p. 79, bottom, the Hoag Collection; pp. 62-63, Jack Abrams; p. 68, Jack Abrams; p. 70, bottom, Jack Abrams; p. 74, the Jacobsen family; p. 80, Florence Bowes; p. 110, John Hulsen; pp. 116-120, Beatrice Teich; pp. 122-130, June Hess Kelly; pp. 134-135, aerial maps, Lockwood, Kessler, Bartlett, Inc., Syosset; p. 136; Jack Abrams; p. 137, map, C. Fleck Enterprises, Huntington. All other photos and maps are courtesy of the Huntington Historical Society, or are from the author's collection.

INDEX

A

B

C

D

E

F

G

H

I

J

K

L

M